BETWEENER AUTOETHNOGRAPHIES

How do we persuade people that we all have common experiences and hopes? That we are ever more dependent on each other in times of globalization via technology, commerce, climate change, and overpopulation? How do we move from an "Us and Them" mentality to simply "Us"?

In this book, a follow-up to their first book *Betweener Talk*, the authors share autoethnographies about being and doing scholarship as betweeners searching for inclusivity. The authors have witnessed an escalation of division in their native Brazil and in the USA, as well as in South America more broadly and Europe – places that had been making steady, albeit slow, progress toward greater inclusion. The book explores identity, interactions, existence, and possibilities in the spaces between "Us" and "Them" to help current and future generations imagine a more inclusive way of living – as Us. It is about how two Third World scholars think the Postcolonial/Decolonizing discourse – with a performance studies lens – can further notions of inclusive social justice through scholarship borne out of lived oppression and the struggle for humanization.

It is a union of two authors who, in their own words "have been close friends since our youth, both captivated by Paulo Freire's notion of education and social transformation through a praxis of conscientização (conscientization), but who experienced life growing up at opposite ends of the social class spectrum. Early through love and later through theory, we have come to viscerally inhabit and embrace our betweener identities in scholarship and daily lives, breaking the distance between us and the paradigms that attempt to separate political, personal, and professional life."

The authors' hope is that their own and other betweener autoethnographies can contribute to the larger qualitative inquiry global movement and its central goal: marching together toward ever greater social justice.

Marcelo Diversi is Professor of Human Development at Washington State University Vancouver. His first book, *Betweener Talk*, also co-authored with Claudio Moreira, won the 2010 Best Book Award from the Ethnography Division of the National Communications Association. He has authored dozens of articles in leading qualitative inquiry journals and won several teaching awards along his career.

Claudio Moreira is Associate Professor of Performance Studies, Department of Communications at the University of Massachusetts Amherst. His first book, *Betweener Talk*, also co-authored with Marcelo Diversi, won the 2010 Best Book Award from the Ethnography Division of the National Communications Association. A specialist in performance autoethnography, he has more than two dozen articles published. In 2016, he won the Distinguished Teaching Award, the most prestigious and only student-oriented teaching award at the University of Massachusetts.

QUALITATIVE INQUIRY AND SOCIAL JUSTICE

Series Editors: Norman K. Denzin and Yvonna Lincoln
University of Illinois at Urbana-Champaign and Texas A&M University

Books in this series address the role of critical qualitative research in an era that cries out for emancipatory visions that move people to struggle and resist oppression. Rooted in an ethical framework that is based on human rights and social justice, the series publishes exemplary studies that advance this transformative paradigm.

Other volumes in this series include:

Globalized Nostalgia
Tourism, Heritage, and the Politics of Place
Christina Ceisel

Betweener Autoethnographies
A Path Towards Social Justice
Marcelo Diversi and Claudio Moreira

Ethnotheatre
Research from Page to Stage
Johnny Saldaña

Autoethnography and the Other
Unsettling Power through Utopian Performatives
Tami Spry

Pedagogy of Solidarity
Paulo Freire, Ana Maria Araujo Freire and Walter de Oliveira

Body, Paper, Stage
Writing and Performing Autoethnography
Tami Spry

For a full list of titles in this series, please visit www.routledge.com/Qualitative-Inquiry-and-Social-Justice/book-series/QISJ

BETWEENER AUTOETHNOGRAPHIES

A Path Towards Social Justice

Marcelo Diversi and Claudio Moreira

NEW YORK AND LONDON

First published 2018
by Routledge
711 Third Avenue, New York, NY 10017

and by Routledge
2 Park Square, Milton Park, Abingdon, Oxon OX14 4RN

Routledge is an imprint of the Taylor & Francis Group, an informa business

© 2018 Taylor & Francis

The right of Marcelo Diversi and Claudio Moreira to be identified as authors of this work has been asserted by him/her/them in accordance with sections 77 and 78 of the Copyright, Designs and Patents Act 1988.

All rights reserved. No part of this book may be reprinted or reproduced or utilised in any form or by any electronic, mechanical, or other means, now known or hereafter invented, including photocopying and recording, or in any information storage or retrieval system, without permission in writing from the publishers.

Trademark notice: Product or corporate names may be trademarks or registered trademarks, and are used only for identification and explanation without intent to infringe.

Library of Congress Cataloging in Publication Data
Names: Diversi, Marcelo, 1967- author. | Moreira, Claudio, 1968- author.
Title: Betweener autoethnographies : a path towards social justice / Marcelo Diversi and Claudio Moreira.
Description: New York, NY : Routledge, 2018. | Series: Qualitative inquiry and social justice | Includes bibliographical references.
Identifiers: LCCN 2017057693 | ISBN 9781138560147 (hbk) | ISBN 9781138560154 (pbk) | ISBN 9780203711996 (ebk)
Subjects: LCSH: Knowledge, Sociology of. | Social justice. | Postcolonialism. | Decolonization. | Qualitative research.
Classification: LCC HM651 .D58 2018 | DDC 303.3/72--dc23
LC record available at https://lccn.loc.gov/2017057693

ISBN: 978-1-138-56014-7 (hbk)
ISBN: 978-1-138-56015-4 (pbk)
ISBN: 978-0-203-71199-6 (ebk)

Typeset in Bembo
by Taylor & Francis Books

To all who have been seeking paths to social justice through unreasonable hope for reconciliation, healing, and unconditional inclusion in the large human family.

CONTENTS

List of figures ix
Series Editor Foreword x
Acknowledgments xii

Introduction 1

PART I
Performing Social Justice 7

1 Expanding the Circle of Us 9
2 Locating Betweener Autoethnographies in Qualitative Inquiry 15

PART II
Betweener Autoethnographies 25

3 Betweenness in Writing and Performativity: Betweeners Speak Up 27
4 Betweenness in Systemic Exclusion: When Janitors Dare to Become Scholars 39
5 Betweenness in Decolonizing Inquiry 83

PART III
Contemporary Issues on Us versus Them 107

6 Betweener Autoethnographies 109

7 Traveling Identities 119

8 Activism through Decolonizing Inquiry 125

References *131*
Index *137*

FIGURES

5.1 Copy of the first page from Pero Vaz de Caminha's letter to King Manuel I of Portugal, signed May 1, 1500, detailing his first arrival in the new land and encounter with its indigenous inhabitants. The letter reads "Eram pardos, todos nus, sem coisa alguma que lhes cobrisse suas vergonhas. Nas mãos traziam arcos com suas setas. Vinham todos rijamente sobre o bater; e Nicolau Coelho lhes fez sinal que pousassem os arcos. E eles os pousaram." (*They were dark-skinned, all naked, without any covering for their shame. They carried bows and arrows in their hands. They came tensely toward the shore; and Nicolau Coelho made a sign for them to put down their bows. And they put them down*)   91

5.2 Chief Raoni   98

SERIES EDITOR FOREWORD

Betweener Autoethnographies: A Path Toward Social Justice is a utopian manifesto. In these troubled divisive times the authors ask: How do we get from Us *versus* Them? To Us *and* Them? Is that possible? If so, how? Here is where we see betweener autoethnographies being, perhaps, useful, hopeful, necessary.

This book is a consensual dialogical collaboration by two Brazilian scholars, working in American academia, who find common ground in an ontological stance that embraces the indivisibility between the study of being and being in and of itself. This book is about rethinking performance autoethnography, about the formation of a critical performative cultural politics, about what happens when everything is already performative, when the dividing line between performativity and performance disappears; they call this betweener autoethnography.

This is a book about what this form of writing means for writers who want to perform work that leads to social justice. It is for writers who have a desire to contribute to a critical discourse that addresses central issues confronting democracy and racism in post-postmodern America, life, narrative, Trump, and melodrama under the auspices of late neoliberal capitalism.

Betweener Autoethnographies: A Path Toward Social Justice stands on the shoulders of its predecessor, the award-winning *Betweener Talk: Decolonizing Knowledge Production, Pedagogy, and Praxis*. It too embraces the dialogical, performance turn in the human disciplines. Thoroughly grounded in the worlds of the colonizer, the dialogue works back and forth across Paulo Freire, Gloria Anzaldua, Soyini Madison, Dwight Conquergood, Mary Weems, Bryant Alexander, Tami Spry, and various Third World feminisms.

Betweener performance autoethnography is a blurred genre. It is many things at the same time. It bends and twists the meanings of ethnography, ethnographer, and performance. There is no separation between the writer, the ethnographer, the performer, and the world. Betweener performance autoethnography makes the writers self-visible through performance, through performance writing, through the writers' presence in the world. Betweener performance autoethnographers are committed to changing the world one word, one performance at a time. The community is global.

Autoethnography is easily confused with other terms. It is not: ethnography, autobiography, biography, personal narrative, personal history, life history, life story, or personal experience story. It works from broad theoretical standpoints but does not privilege theory over visceral experience. It is more than personal writing or cultural critique. It is more than performance. But it is performative. It is transgressive. It is resistance. It is dialogical. It is ethical. It is political, personal, embodied, collaborative, imaginative, artistic, creative, a form of intervention, a plea for social justice. Clearly this discourse is not standing still. Writing selves are performing new writing practices, blurring fact and fiction, challenging the dividing line between performer and performed, observer and observed.

After Marcelo and Claudio, I too seek a critical autoethnographic betweener discourse. This requires a productive dialogue between indigenous and critical (race) scholars. It involves a revisioning of critical pedagogy, a regrounding of Paulo Freire's pedagogy of the oppressed in local, indigenous contexts. It understands that all inquiry is political and moral. It confronts the tension between the Western critical theory paradigm and indigenous knowledge, theory, and praxis. It uses methods critically, for explicit social justice purposes. It values the transformative power of indigenous, subjugated knowledges. It values the local pedagogical practices that produce these knowledges. At the same time it studies the political, ethical, and aesthetic technologies that transform the practices of indigeneity into marketable commodities and performances. It seeks forms of praxis and inquiry that are emancipatory, collaborative, and empowering. The critical betweener performance scholar is an allied Other. Marcelo and Claudio show us how to be this way.

There has never been a greater need for a militant utopianism which will help us imagine a world free of conflict, terror, and death, a world that is caring, loving, truly compassionate, a world that honors healing and difference. This powerful book helps us imagine our way into this space.

Norman K. Denzin

ACKNOWLEDGMENTS

In our second endeavor
Certain things are different and yet
Certain things remain
The pleasure of feeling grateful . . .
We couldn't have done it alone, and we are very thankful for the support and encouragement by Norman Denzin, Hannah Shakespeare, Matt Bickerton
Inspired by Anzaldúa and Paulo Freire
And
By those who honor differences
People who put their bodies in the line of fire for ideals of social justice
Bodies that make impossibilities possible
Brothers and sisters everywhere working to advance decolonizing pedagogies
People who have touched our lives, who make hope indispensable
Dani, Analua, Francisco, Sylvinha, Drica, Sherekao
To my brother Marcelo
To my brother Claudio
To all interested in expanding a sense of Us
Betweeners for inclusive dreams of social justice, democracy, liberty
Together we are a force
We resist because we must, there are no other options
As our muse says
Onward!

We also want to acknowledge the presses in which previously published manuscripts appeared in full or in part: the University of California Press, for

"When janitors dare to become scholars" and "Betweeners speak up"; Sage, for "Classrooms as decolonizing sites," "Dismantling the myth of the lone expert," and "Performing betweener autoethnographies"; Taylor & Francis, for "Decolonizing constructions of childhood" and "Missing bodies"; and Peter Lang Publishing, for "Migrant stories."

INTRODUCTION

How do we get from Us *versus* Them to Us *and* Them?
Is that possible?
If so, how?
If not, how close to it can we get?
How do we get from Us *versus* Them to *just* Us?
Is that possible?
If so, how?
If not, how do we keep on trying anyway?
These questions are more urgent, more pressing than ever
Our survival depends on our ability to expand the notion of Us
The circle of Us
The spaces between Us and Them need to be filled with compassion over hatred
With cooperation over non-zero sum propositions
With stories where We resonate with Their humanity, and vice versa
We have a long and hard road ahead
Alone, despair seems inevitable, paralyzing
Together, we might be able to keep Our bearings toward social justice
In times of increasing Us versus Themism
In times of greater exclusionary politics
In times when hope for social justice seems to have lost its way

★★★

We have been witnessing an escalation of Us versus Themism in Brazil, where we grew up, in the U.S.A., where we live and labor, in our South American neighbors, in our European allies, in places that have been making steady, albeit slow for those on the wrong side of the track, progress toward greater inclusion since the middle of the last century. The rise of the global right, founded on notions of purity of race, culture, religion, and traditional gender binaries, is palpable in the political success of parties with anti-immigration crusades, with the rise of populist nationalism based on a narrative of "a need to take care of our own," with renewed attacks on LGBTQ+ individuals and communities, with a disingenuous narrative linking civil war refugees with organized terrorist organizations, with fear-mongering stories of the Other.

In the U.S.A., Donald Trump won a presidential election by inflaming the notion of Us *versus* Them. They are rapists and criminals, he said about Mexican immigrants. He is not a war hero, he said of Senator John McCain, because Trump doesn't like soldiers captured in battle. He said he could see blood coming out of Megyn Kelly's eyes, he could see "blood coming out of her wherever," when she asked him questions about his misogynistic comments on women throughout his public years. Trump repeated his claim, during his presidential campaign, that he could see Muslims in New Jersey celebrating the 9/11 attacks. "It did happen. I saw it. It was on television," he claimed. On the Syrian refugees crisis, Trump made fellow humans who lost their homes, families, cities, jobs, careers, country, and a deep sense of belonging into a flat stereotype of *them*: "I don't want the people from Syria coming in, because we don't know who they are. We don't know who they are. And I don't want them coming in." Trump has called, in public and with documented records, Blacks lazy, saying that laziness is a trait in Blacks, "it really is, I believe that. It is not anything they can control" (O'Donnell, 1991). Trump has made fun of a disabled journalist who was critical of him. He single-handedly birthed and raised a movement to delegitimize Barack Obama as President of the United States on the premise that Obama was not an American citizen, was not one of Us. And after Obama produced his birth certificate, Trump attempted to delegitimize him as intelligent enough to have gone to an Ivy League university, gotten a law degree, or written a book on his own (Coates, 2017). Trump has twisted the Take a Knee movement in the National Football Association from a protest against racial inequality in America, and undisputable fact, and made it into an Us versus Them issue. According to this approach, if you take a knee during the national anthem, you are against Us, against America, against soldiers, against the flag, against patriotism, against the sport itself. Not being upset about the actual point of protest, racial inequality, in the Take a Knee movement is, in and of itself, a clear expression of white supremacy in the U.S. And supremacy ideologies are founded in the hostile notion of Us versus Them. It could not thrive in a cooperative notion of Us and Them. It could not exist if humanity got to the point of realizing there is no Them in our globalized, technological, warming, and overpopulated times.

Trump and his supporters have magnified the adversarial notion of Us versus Them in domestic and international communities with their American First boastings, unilateral exit from international agreements on nuclear power, trade, climate, and the sustainability of planet earth. Trump has called for the annihilation of entire countries, such as North Korea and Iran, if they don't toe his line and fully submit. Nuclear war has suddenly become a real threat again in the divisive wake of Us versus Them narratives and shouts. That, and much more along the Us versus Them ideological and rhetorical lines, is what his campaign meant by Make America Great Again. Stoke Us versus Themisms and you are likely to divide people along race lines. It worked for his presidential campaign. Across all classes, education levels, geographical location, age groups, even gender, Trump won the majority of White votes. He is not alone in the Us versus Them frame of mind. He represents a large portion of the American obsession with Us versus Themisms, at least 62,984,825 Americans, or 46.09 percent of those who voted in 2016 (Federal Elections Commission, 2017).

The list of narratives that stoke polarizing notions of Us versus Them is long, intense, and so outrageous that most people seem too overwhelmed to counter-argue every wedge pounded between Us and Them. Even worse for social justice and humanistic notions is the fact that the Us versus Them ideology Trump represents and leads is in control of the greatest political and ideological platform of our times, the White House and its control of the most massive financial and military power in the world. The (re)turn toward ideologies of domination and exclusion imperils everyone and anyone outside of their very narrow circle of Us, and it is not confined to the U.S.A.

We also saw the rise of the global right and their Us versus Them agendas in the United Kingdom with Brexit, which was mostly supported by anti-immigrant sentiments, and a series of similar nationalist parties rising again in Western Europe. Populist narratives of cultural purity and tradition have been used as justification for violence against the Other in nations that worked hard to unify and create economic cooperation after the two world wars of the 20th century. And so we (re)turn to a combative and hostile ideology of Us versus Them in the second decade of the 21st century, just when we needed the opposite, an expansion of the circle of Us. Globally, humanity's situation is not ideal, to say the least.

Take the plight of refugees of climate change and civil war conflict, for instance: "The number of refugees, asylum-seekers and internally displaced people around the world has topped 65 million," the United Nations High Commissioner on Refugees announced in the summer of 2016.

> One in every 113 people on Earth has now been driven from their home by persecution, conflict and violence or human rights violations. Two other ways to wrap your mind around that number: Each minute, 24 people around the world flee their home because of violence or persecution. And if the world's displaced people were their own nation, it would be larger than the United Kingdom.
>
> *(Domonoske, 2016)*

Take the violence carried against the Other, against Them, in the wake of Brexit and the Trump presidential campaign. Jo Cox, a 41-year-old woman, mother of two young children, a member of the UK Parliament, was shot and stabbed to death, outside a library in Leeds, UK, killed by a man who apparently shouted "Britain First!" during and after the attack, a few days before the country's referendum over whether to stay or leave the European Union. Britain First is a right-wing group that often stages provocative anti-Muslim demonstrations in the UK. Jo Cox had won an election as a member of the Labour Party after a long career in humanitarian work and her outspoken support for Syrian civilians and refugees.

★★★

We see the raising of walls all over Europe against desperate refugees of war in Syria and northern African lands and wonder if there wasn't a way to raise open arms instead.

★★★

Closer to our other home, Brazil, where we were born, raised, and became brothers in joy, hope, and love, we have seen a strong (re)turn to a dominant ideology of Us versus Them, of hostility against the Other, of exclusion, of lame excuses for development at the cost of lives and ecological systems. We see the soft coup in Brazil against a democratically elected president from the Worker's Party, Dilma Rousseff, the first female president of our motherland, and wonder if a male president would have been impeached under the same circumstances. We wonder if a member of the historical Brazilian elite would have been called stupid, dumb, and ignorant in public, and with such insistence. We wonder how people who blamed Dilma Rousseff for everything wrong with Brazil could so easily believe the Us-versus-Them propaganda spun by the corporate media giants. We wonder how protests against Dilma Rousseff and the Worker's Party included protests against Paulo Freire and his pedagogy of the oppressed. How can anyone protest against liberation and humanization of those historically oppressed? By making Them, the historically oppressed, seem innately different from Us, less than Us, ungrateful for the meager handouts thrown Their way, by making Them a menace to Us.

★★★

Back in the U.S.A. As we were talking about the news, the world, our work together, our teaching, our lives, our friendship, our beloved ones, our unknown brothers and sisters, we heard about the Orlando shooting, the 49 people who were shot dead, the 53 people who were injured, the 102 families who were immediately dragged into horror by a 29-year-old man who was able to legally buy weapons of war for personal use.

Why did the shooter want to kill people dancing and having fun at a nightclub?

Why did he target a gay club?

Why did he call 911 and pledge allegiance to ISIS?

Why did he post about his allegiance to extremists groups like ISIS, Hezbollah, and Al-Qaeda, who are at war with each other?

Why was the shooter a regular client at Pulse before his rampage?

Why was the shooter a user of gay dating apps?

We don't have ways to answer these questions now. And even the investigators and prosecutors pouring over intelligence about the shooter's virtual life won't, likely, get the full picture, however long they dig. But it is clear to us that hatred toward the Other is at the center of his imaginations, decisions, and acts leading to the Pulse massacre.

Us versus Them

Us and Them

Who is Us?

Who is Them?

What narratives create and reify these circles?

Who creates and reifies these circles of inclusion and exclusion?

For whose profit?

At whose expense?

The visual distance between Us and Them seems small to us

The linguistic distance between Us and Them seems a lot wider

The geographical distance between Us and Them seems irrelevant

At least in our hyper migrant realities and lived experiences

But the imaginary distance between Us and Them feels gargantuan to us

That is where we see betweener autoethnographies being, perhaps, useful

Hopeful

Necessary

PART I
Performing Social Justice

1
EXPANDING THE CIRCLE OF US

How do we move more people, younger generations in particular, to see all humans as brothers and sisters, with common experiences and hopes, ever more dependent on each other in times of globalization via technology, commerce, climate change, and overpopulation? We write and teach with this question as a central guide. We see the betweener experience, the moments in which we find ourselves labeled as dehumanized Others based on flat exclusionary stereotypes, as a common ground where we can all meet in ever kinder and more cooperative, inclusive ways. We think that the recognition of oneself in the excluded Other has been central in the successful inclusionary movements and moments in history. We think that autoethnographies exploring identity, interactions, existence, and possibilities in the spaces *between* Us *and* Them can help current and future generations imagine an ever expanding circle of Us when, over time, there will be no more Them, at least not in dehumanizing, exclusionary ways. As James Baldwin stated decades ago "We've got to be as clear-headed about human beings as possible, because we are still each other's only hope" (Mead & Baldwin, 1972, p. 45). We have been on earth long enough to recognize that our tribal tendencies may never be tamed, permanently erased, or even temporarily exiled. But we also see, in our personal lives, in our classrooms, in the responses to our writing, and in the humanist thinkers who came before us, on whose shoulders we stand, the transforming possibilities for hope and greater justice, in tireless search for the common humanity that diminishes the spaces between Us and Them, between inclusion and exclusion, between kindness and hatred, between joy and pain, between liberation and oppression, between cooperation and greed, between compassion and indifference.

We build upon our first book together, *Betweener Talk* (2009), sharing some of the betweener autoethnographies we have written since, and revisiting writers and their ideas about liberation, dreams of inclusion, and imaginations about ontological hope. Inspired by Paulo Freire and his *Pedagogy of Hope* (1995), we have been teaching, writing, and collaborating believing that "[h]ope is an ontological need, (p. 8)" perhaps even more so now that many democracies are experiencing a return to populist nationalism, full of intense and overt exclusionary narratives and unfriendly walls, founded on ideologies and narratives that intensify notions of Us against Them along ethnic, gender, class, sexual orientation, (dis) abilities, religious and immigration status. We have also (re)turned to the writings of Frederick Douglass for inspiration, comfort, guidance, and, above all, historical perspective. We have found ourselves in a state of hopelessness in recent times, seeing the proverbial pendulum swinging hard toward a politics of exclusion at the expense of the humanity in the Other. Hopelessness is but hope that has lost its bearings, to paraphrase Paulo Freire (1995/2004). And we have gone back to Frederick Douglass' narratives of an American slave in order to regain historical perspective in the long human struggle against oppressive systems based on Us versus Them ideologies. Douglass found a way to keep hope for justice and human rights while facing institutionalized slavery, while being a slave himself, while suffering and witnessing violence that no White master of the time could ever accept for their worst enemies – as long as they were White, of course.

> From my earliest recollection, I date the entertainment of a deep conviction that slavery would not always be able to hold me within its foul embrace; and in the darkest hours of my career in slavery, this living word of faith and spirit of hope departed not from me, but remained like ministering angels to cheer me through the gloom.
>
> *(1845/2003, p. 39)*

In our less hopeful days, we find inspiration and renewed hope in thinking of Douglass, and the countless Others that he represents and whose stories we never got a chance to hear or read, finding ways to keep the faith and spirit of hope alive in slavery, the most profound instantiation of Us versus Them ideology known to humanity. We need his spirit and angels ministering over US all in this time of gloom. And we hear the same from our students and readers. We clearly don't have the answer or clear paths to navigate the contemporary Us versus Them gloom, but we can offer our own attempts to survive, to keep hope alive.

Exploring how betweener autoethnographies can help us find common ground in the spaces between Us and Them is the central theme of this book. We hope that it can help us imagine new and renewed ways to create a larger circle of Us, however insurmountable that may appear from anyone's particular, personal position. We also hope that betweener autoethnographies can contribute to the larger qualitative inquiry of global movement and its central goal: marching together toward ever greater social justice. We will be discussing our framework and methodology for betweener autoethnographies throughout the next chapters.

For now, we want to give the reader a sense of who we are and where our interest in betweener autoethnographies comes from.

In a general sense, this book is about how two Third World scholars think the postcolonial/decolonizing discourse – with a performance studies lens – can further notions of inclusive social justice through scholarship borne out of lived experiences of oppression, borne out of the struggle for humanization among excluded human kinds, and borne out of our experiences with the exclusionary politics of knowledge production in the USA. It is a result of our ongoing performance autoethnography through the identity and geopolitical borders we cross, in the places we live and labor. A central question of our work and the essays in this book is around the possibilities of overcoming hostile notions of Us versus Them, and, ultimately, how we can challenge and decrease the distances that separate Us and Them. We believe that autoethnographic performances of betweener experiences may help all of us in that direction. We think autoethnographies exploring identity, interactions, existence, and possibilities of the spaces *between* Us *and* Them can help current and future generations imagine an ever expanding circle of Us, even to the point where, over time, there will be less *Themisms*, at least not in dehumanizing, exclusionary ways.

This book, as it happens in our work together, offers an angle we believe to be unique in decolonizing inquiry. The story we tell is grounded on a union of two authors who have been close friends since our youth, both captivated by Paulo Freire's notion of education and social transformation through a praxis of conscientização (conscientization), while experiencing life growing up at opposite ends of the social class spectrum. In Brazil, as in most nation-states of our times, this is not an easy barrier to break and overcome. Class is not an easy border to cross. Claudio and Marcelo should not have been friends. Professor Diversi should not have honored visceral knowledge of oppression. Claudio should have been a janitor and therefore a "Professor Moreira" should not have existed at all. Early through love and later through theory, we have come to viscerally inhabit and embrace our betweener identities in scholarship and daily lives, breaking the distance between us and the paradigms that attempt to separate political, personal, and professional life. We perform, teach, and write our academic lives from that space. Hence, we offer our betweener autoethnographic accounts as instantiations of our theoretical ideas about how social sciences inquiry can use self-reflexivity, visceral knowledge, and authorial situatedness to advance scholarship that calls to, and hopes for, more inclusive imaginations of social justice.

We follow Gloria Anzaldua's notion of the postcolonial critique, the notion of betweeners who destabilize the relationship between center and periphery, who hope to create space for resistance and transformation through the inclusion of first-hand visceral knowledge of oppression in the classroom and academic scholarship. This book is a consensual dialogical collaboration by two Brazilian scholars, working in American academia, who find common ground in an ontological stance that embraces the indivisibility between the study of being and being in and of itself.

Autoethnographies that explore the in-between spaces have grown out of our personal experiences and our understanding of theories and narratives of conscientization. Autoethnographies of the in-between are the result of our dialogue about the roles of academic discourse in relation to systems of oppression that continue to marginalize humans in poverty, in deprivation, in lesser categories, in Them. It is a textual representation of our authorial critique about the disembodied ways in which oppression continues to be constructed, and the ways it is ultimately justified for the benefit of a powerful minority who depends on a hostile gap between Us and Them.

We spend a lot of time living, thinking, acting, and imagining more inclusive possibilities of being in the space between Us and Them, in the history of Us versus Them, sick of the justifications for exclusionary everything, exclusionary anything. We know that we don't have a unique or special insight into humanity. All we can do is offer our thoughts on how to resist the strong (re)turn to Us versus Themism of our times, thoughts on how to move toward greater unity through stories highlighting the human experience of life in-between, thoughts on how to bring resistance and hope and transformative activism to classrooms, to knowledge production. We hope our words and thoughts invite you, the reader, to feel more connected to our common human plights, to our universal desire to live good lives.

Outline of the Rest of the Book

In Chapter 2, we locate our betweener autoethnographies, and its performative autoethnographic model, within the tradition of qualitative inquiry in general, and in the field of critical personal narratives in particular. We also state our ontological and epistemological standpoint in the construction of our vision of betweener autoethnographies as a way of knowing, being, and teaching.

Part II, Betweener Autoethnographies, is a compilation of our work together, our betweener autoethnographies written in the years since *Betweener Talk*, our first book together. This part is divided into three chapters, each with common and interrelated themes: Betweenness in writing and performativity, betweenness in systemic exclusion, and betweenness in decolonizing inquiry. We acknowledge that this organization is somewhat arbitrary. At the same time that these written performances are grouped together in a singular theme, every single text in our manuscript carries the main concepts of this book: A long-term collaborative writing project to create scholarship that starts from love, friendship, a Freirian pedagogy of hope, and where we write our betweener bodies and our experiences of betweenness in search of paths to social justice, through reconciliation and healing. All these performance texts are in close dialogue and connection of one and another.

In Chapter 3, we focus on why we write together, and how this form of writing challenges and resists the neoliberal regime of education so pervasive in our society, and at the same time, offers an alternative model in academic knowledge production that negates the idea of the lone ethnographer as the privileged way of writing. In this chapter, we attempt to advance collaborative writing as a decolonizing form of inquiry that allows us to break away from the expert isolationist writing standpoint and expand our own imaginations of and possibilities for inquiry. We write with an invitation for those with visceral experience of oppression to collaborate with the learned and cultured in the creation of knowledge that heals.

Chapter 4 pays close attention to the exclusion of bodies inside and outside academic walls. We believe that subjugated bodies continue to be missing from classrooms, faculty meetings, high administration, and educational structures everywhere. Talking back to power structures, we try to bond the exclusion of bodies with the exclusion of visceral knowledge in order to contest taken-for-granted notions of what kinds of bodies and knowledges belong inside our classrooms and universities. Can a janitor be a scholar? Are marginalized humans relegated to a subordinate position of research subject in the process of knowledge production? Where are the excluded bodies in the production of knowledge about oppression? Where is the untheorized visceral experience of everyday discrimination? We keep demanding space for visceral knowledge of oppression to advance decolonizing discourses that may lead to more inclusive notions of social justice.

In Chapter 5, we focus our attention on how we attempt to examine, challenge, and resist neoliberal dehumanizing narratives of the Other in our classrooms and history books. We insist that the Western systems of knowledge production need to be placed as the object of inquiry, placed at the end of the autoethnographic gaze: We do research while criticizing it. What can we, intellectuals, do to help transform the world outside academic towers? What do we tell children when they ask about what happened to the natives? We bring constructions of childhood and history right into the center of this critique. We bring our bodies as teachers into our writing, using our betweener encounters in the classroom to deconstruct the contemporary narratives of Us versus Them.

In Part III, we write about our thoughts on how to write our history interlaced with the histories of so many oppressed humans, examining our personal histories in relation to so many singularities and shared universalities in the world we hope to see one day, while also imagining how we can aim to become scholar-activists in the classroom and in knowledge production in the tradition of qualitative inquiry. In Chapter 6, we return to our vision for betweener autoethnographies to discuss the theoretical and methodological framework informing our autoethnographic performances and forms of representation. In Chapter 7, we write about our attempts to use betweener autoethnographies as a way of being and writing ourselves into the history of resistance against oppression, injustice, and exclusion, starting from our common humanity in betweener identities. We trouble the fixed notions of identity that keep preventing us from including Them in the same category of humanity we attribute to those we perceive as part of Us.

In Chapter 8, we perform our final act of this book. We try to show that in creating decolonizing performances, written (in the form of articles, books) and embodied (on the stage of the classroom and academic conferences), we are challenging the "traditional" construction of scientific knowledge and, at the same time, broadening the notion of what an intellectual activist may be. Can/should a professor be an activist? What happens when our decolonizing (conscious effort to break the colonial treaty) bodies and performance texts invade the mostly White space of academic classrooms and scholarly texts? What possibilities may such acts create? We end with our thoughts on how betweener autoethnographies can be acts of activism toward social justice and an expanded circle of Us.

2
LOCATING BETWEENER AUTOETHNOGRAPHIES IN QUALITATIVE INQUIRY

What we have been calling betweener autoethnography comes from a long tradition of self-reflexive writing that explores personal experiences and how these experiences connect autobiography to history (Denzin, 1997), how personal individual experiences connect with wider cultural, political, and social understandings (Ellis, 2004). Before it was called autoethnography, however, the central importance of connecting the personal to the political had been very clear to those enslaved and otherwise conquered, colonized, and historically dehumanized. As literacy itself was withheld from the oppressed until recent years in human history, we have known of this critical form of personal narrative only from oral traditions, folklore, and various arts. We think that Frederick Douglass, for instance, through his three autobiographical narratives (Douglass, 1845, 1855, 1881), was an earlier writer of personal narratives used directly to critique, trouble, resist, and challenge systems of oppression, while also making a call to liberation, freedom, emancipation, and, ultimately, reconciliation and social healing. We intend the same with our own betweener autoethnographies in the early part of the 21st century, with our own contemporary critical personal narratives about oppressive Us versus Themisms, with a call for unconditional inclusion of the Other in a utopian circle of Us. As we try to imagine and constantly revive notions of utopia and paths to a kinder and more just world for more people, we have gone back in time to find renewed inspiration in these earlier critical storytellers.

In our view, folks like Frederick Douglass and Harriet Tubman told critical stories of oppression, hope against all odds, and liberation in 1800s North America. Paulo Freire, Eduardo Galeano, liberation theologists from South America, Franz Fanon, Edward Said, Homi Bhabha, to cite a few of the more prominent figures informing our betweener autoethnographies, spent a large portion of the 20th century writing critical narratives against systems of oppression from their own personal standpoints and biographies. Third World and Black feminists like Audrey Lorde, Gloria Anzaldua, and bell hooks reminded us, so very vividly in the same period, that they had been writing self-reflexive personal narratives as cultural critique long before autoethnography became a recognizable and distinct form of ethnography in the late 1990s and early 2000s in Western academia. All of these earlier thinkers, writers, activists, and educators have been writing about the political from the personal standpoint with the urgency of those who depend on it — that is, making the personal political, talking back to the oppressors' version of history — for survival within the dominant patriarchal White supremacist Western ideology.

Although we trace our ontological, epistemological, and ethical roots to these earlier origins of critical personal narratives of inquiry and activism, we also greatly appreciate and acknowledge the autoethnographic foundations laid out by our contemporaries in more recent years. Deriving from the established ethnographic method used in anthropology and sociology to observe, label, and map culture and its practices, autoethnography evolved in the midst of the crisis of representation of Western social sciences in the 1970s, 1980s, and 1990s. It had to evolve in order to address the poststructural and postmodern challenges to positivism's refusal to acknowledge the importance of examining authorial positionality, subjectivity, reflexivity, and politics, its refusal to turn the politics of knowledge production into a central object of inquiry in and of itself (Clifford & Marcus, 1986; Denzin & Lincoln, 1994; Geertz, 1973; Kincheloe & McLaren, 1994). In the wake of postmodernism and poststructuralism came greater experimentation with authorship, positionality, self-reflexivity, subjectivity, and various forms of critical takes on more traditional lenses in social sciences and humanities (Turner & Bruner, 1986). The blurring of disciplinary and paradigmatic boundaries opened the gates wider for the blending of ethnography with poetics, performance, autobiographies, cultural studies, and critical studies of race, gender, and colonization.

Autoethnography today is not a singular or novel qualitative form of inquiry. And, as with all human storytelling and forms of inquiry about lived experiences, its origins and stories of birth are surely more complex and layered than what we can and want to examine in this book. The relatively new field of autoethnography already has several detailed accounts and histories, with its own Handbook of Autoethnography (Holman Jones, Adams, & Ellis, 2013), and several tomes dedicated to its history and place in qualitative inquiry (Denzin, 2003, 2013; Ellis, 2004; Spry, 2016), to practical applications and internal tensions between analytical and evocative forms of autoethnography (Bochner & Ellis, 2016) and extensive collections of topics and styles (Adams, Holman Jones, & Ellis, 2015). So we follow in the footsteps of several fellow autoethnographers (e.g., Douglas & Carless, 2013; Spry, 2016) who acknowledge the many histories of autoethnography and attempt to offer a glimpse into how we came about autoethnography, and where we ground the ontological, epistemological, and ethical foundations of our betweener focus.

Initially, this form of writing, thinking, and living came to Marcelo through the encounter between critical theory, poststructuralism, and postcolonialism with the postmodernist ethnographies of the 1980s. To Claudio, initially it came through poetic performance and resistance against the crushing brutality of social class. In addition to our unlikely friendship across static class divides in Brazil, we shared youthful interpretations of anti-colonial theories and artistic expressions of liberation. And we shared a fire in the belly to spend our adult lives in the cause of social justice. We write extensively about our earlier connections and subsequent intellectual collaborations elsewhere (Diversi & Moreira, 2009), but the central point here is that we each brought our shared Freirian ideals and our distinct class experiences to our ethnographies. Marcelo started through critical ethnographies (1998) and Claudio through performance ethnographies (2008). As we have worked together through the last many years, we have converged into autoethnographies that focus on using our experiences of living in-between identities and (dis)locations to examine systems of oppression that feed widespread ideologies of Us versus Them, while searching for pedagogical and performing ways to bring, through stories of exclusion that at some point or another touches every human, reconciliation and healing to the spaces between Us and Them. Thus, betweener autoethnographies: Autoethnographies that make the spaces in-between Us and Them the object of inquiry in our scholarship, pedagogy, and praxis.

In addition to the historical roots we describe above, we also find epistemological inspiration and guidance in Denzin's autoethnographic project (2013, p. ix) and its foundation on C. Wright Mills' (1959) sociological imagination, Jean Paul Sartre's (1981) universal singular, and Jacques Derrida's (1967/2016) metaphysics of presence. We also attempt to write from our universal singularities, our Third World scholar identities, to put history and biography together, to move from personal troubles to public issues. Like other forms of critical and political autoethnographies, we attempt to write representations of our betweener bodies, our lived experiences, situated in relation to the politics of exclusion of everyday life and knowledge production, about our encounters with dehumanization, exclusion, lives lived between Us and Them, lives that seem to beg for inclusion in the circle of Us, away from the demonizing or invisible or meaningless or untouchable Them.

Like many other forms of autoethnography, we lean on the relational possibilities of performing betweenness. Like many other forms of autoethnography, we start our writings from the body, the flesh wounded by oppression. But unlike autoethnographies that center on the personal without making direct connections and critique of the political in which the personal lives and experiences live, we see betweener autoethnographies always writing from and existing in – ontologically, epistemologically, ethically – critical gaze at the political systems of oppression creating and sustaining stories of Us versus Them. As James Baldwin reminds all of us,

> You write in order to change the world, knowing perfectly well that you probably can't, but also knowing that literature is indispensable to the world... The world changes according to the way people see it, and if you alter, even but a millimeter the way people look at reality, then you can change it.
>
> *(1979, p. 3)*

In this sense, we join forces with bell hooks when she considers the possibility that the academy may be able to "produce theory that begins with the experiential before it enters the printed stage" (1989, p. 36). Joni Jones' words also resonate with the type of autoethnography we attempt to write: "Performance work in the academy subverts the mind/body split even while it appears to exist on the physical end of that inappropriate binary, because performance is at once physical and intellectual, visceral and cerebral" (Jones, 1997, p. 60). We write autoethnographies that attempt to value bodies, honor visceral knowledge of oppression as much and prior to theoretical knowledge of oppression, and that is always deconstructing political ideologies of Us versus Them.

Performance Turn

> I'll lay my cards on the table. We need a performance studies paradigm that understands performance simultaneously as a form of inquiry and as a form of activism, as critique, as critical citizenship. I seek a critical sociological imagination that inspires and empowers persons to act on their utopian impulses. These moments and their performances are etched in history, memory, dreams, hope, pain, resistance, and joy.
>
> *(Norman Denzin, 2010, p. 18)*

As important to our betweener autoethnographies is the performance turn (Denzin, 2003). In 1991, Dwight Conquergood wrote what is considered a classic in performance studies, "Rethinking Ethnography." There, he traces the growing of performance theory into ethnography to Victor Turner's (1986) ontological concept, then subversive, of "humankind as homo-performers – a culture-inventing, social-performing, self-making, and self-transforming creature" (p. 187), moving the field away from "preoccupations with universal system, structure, form, and towards particular practices, people, and performances" (p. 187). It marks the return to the body, the living, creative, suffering, imaginative bodies of human beings trying to make sense of life in the places they live and labor. Building upon Conquergood's notion of the movement from performance as imitation (mimesis) to performance as an aesthetic construction (poesies) to performance as an intervention (kinesis) betweener autoethnographies inhabit the space where performance (the done) and performative (the doing) collide in the moment of the performance (written or embodied) in the performer's (writer's) body, trying to recover the "saying" from the "said" (Conquergood, 1991).

Using Della Pollock's words:

> I want to claim more power for performance: to think about the tension between the thing done and doing as a collision of past and present producing the excess of what's as yet undone, what's yet to be done. I want to think about how performance propels us forward into a future world, a world full of dangerous and fantastic possibilities.
>
> *(Pollock, 2007, p. 243)*

We also see the "performative I" bringing more power in connecting with audiences through our autoethnographic writing and teaching. Betweener autoethnography is a form of intervention with the clear intention to demonstrate both its performativity and to unsettle power dynamics in the world (Spry, 2016). We try to write and perform our moral acts, we try to help the creation of imaginations about a future of more inclusive possibilities, while also trying to resist and challenge the present dangers (Denzin & Giardina, 2013).

In addition, performance gives us the possibility of bringing to our autoethnography scholars and theories that we often don't see in more analytical forms of autoethnography. In performing our betweener autoethnographies, we see more possibilities in breaking disciplinary binaries and creating spaces for qualitative inquiry that touches and moves audiences into action, or at least into thinking more inclusively. In the words of Conquergood:

> The ongoing challenge of performance studies is to refuse and supersede this deeply entrenched division of labor, apartheid of knowledges, that plays out inside the academy as the difference between thinking and doing, interpreting and making, conceptualizing and creating. The division of labor between theory and practice, abstraction and embodiment, is an arbitrary and rigged choice, and, like all binarisms, it is booby-trapped.
>
> *(2002, p. 153)*

Within the field of performance studies, our understanding/version of autoethnography is situated in the intersections of Third World feminism, postcolonialism, cultural studies, and critical pedagogy (Denzin, 2003; Pineau, 1998). It works to destabilize and subvert the supremacy in the dichotomies of body and mind, theory and practice, personal and political, researcher and subject so pervasive in academic settings, opening up, creating doors into the in-between spaces of our everyday lives (Spry, 2016). Again, the words of Joni L. Jones become essential to us: "Performance may be theorized about, but theory of the performance is imbedded in the performance itself, 'flaws' and all. The provocative question is not 'What theory created this performance?' but 'What theory is revealed through this performance?'" (Jones, 1997, p. 55). And so, how do we write our betweener lives? Again, Jones provides everyday life possibilities: "In this writing I am very much in my body as I am in performance as I am in everyday life" (Jones, 1997, p. 58).

Together with inserting our bodies in our research writing, performance studies provides us with yet another tool to create possible answers to the crises of representation. Della Pollock (1998a, 1998b) connects the act of writing with embodied scholarship, with the body typing the words, delineating possibilities for performative writing as evocative, metonymic, subjective, nervous, citational, and consequential,

> it operates by synaptic relay, drawing one charged moment into another, constituting knowledge in an ongoing process of transmission and referral, finding in the wide-ranging play of textuality an urgency that keeps what amounts to textual travel from lapsing into tourism, and that binds the traveler to his/her surging course like an electrical charge to its conduit.
> (Pollock, 1998a, p. 91)

Suddenly, through the performance turn, it was possible for us to spill our guts, writing our visceral experiences of our bodies into pages that seem to tremble when we perform our autoethnographies. Performance writing wasn't appealing to us because it is written differently from a more conventional form, but because it insisted that we engage in writing that is shaped by both loss and hopeful possibilities, forms of autoethnography that "pushes the limits of textual epistemologies" (Pollock, 1998b, p. 44).

Critical Pedagogy

We feel that we are intellectual children of Paulo Freire by culture, language, geography, and time. His seminal work, *Pedagogy of the Oppressed* (1970), has been essential to our lives for decades. The later work on the *Pedagogy of Hope* (2004), where Freire revisited his classic *Pedagogy of the Oppressed*, became a sacred fountain of inspiration in our coming together, so many times, over and over again, to write betweener autoethnographies. He gave us language to name a sensation we had been carrying around in our gut when he wrote that hope is an ontological necessity. We build our teaching philosophy and collaborative autoethnographies upon Freire's concept of liberatory education, on conscientização, a praxis that focuses on the development of critical consciousness, a dialogical process through which cultural workers guide students in becoming critical thinkers by examining the origin and use of knowledge and, similar to Mills' notion of sociological imagination (Mills, 1959), invites the Other to bring history and biography together in order to understand their own lots. Freire's conscientization has empowered us to recognize and write about relations between our individual experiences and the social contexts in which these lived experiences were shaped, the culture in which our betweener identities and bodies were raised and marked. It has helped us name and write about our class differences from the beginning of our friendship to the present academic collaborations. We don't have a way of knowing if Paulo Freire himself would see value in our betweener autoethnographies as a path to his concept of conscientization. But we hope so, for it has helped us become more conscious of our own Us versus Themisms. And as Freire conceptualized conscientization, as a liberatory form of education, we see betweener autoethnographies committed to examining and challenging hegemonic practices/performances that blame inequalities on individual lack of effort – a hegemonic and simplistic practice that tends to diverge criticism away from systemic discrimination in educational settings across the USA, Brazil, and beyond, perpetuating the Us versus Them dominant positionalities.

Third World Feminism

> When I write, it feels like I'm carving bone. It feels like I'm creating my own face, my own heart – a Nahuatl concept. My soul makes itself through the creative act. It is constantly remaking and giving birth to itself in my body.
> (Gloria Anzaldúa, 1987/1999, p. 95)

> The struggle is inner. Chicano, indio, American Indian, mojado, Mexicano, immigrant Latino, Anglo in power, working class Anglo, Black, Asian – our psyches resemble the bordertowns and are populated by the same people. The struggle has always been inner, and is played out in the outer terrains. Awareness of our situation must come before inner changes, which in turn come before changes in society. Nothing happens in the "real" world unless it first happens in the images in our heads.
> *(Gloria Anzaldúa, 1987/1999, p. 109)*

We also draw insight and inspiration in the work of Third World scholarship, particularly of Gloria Anzaldúa and Emma Perez, as we write and perform betweener autoethnographies. Our concept of "Betweeners" comes in large part from them (for more on this, see Diversi & Moreira, 2009, pp. 18–27). Emma Perez suggests that divergent thinking comes from people who arise out of interstitial places, the spaces in-between, the "decolonial imaginary" (Perez, 1999), places in the colonized body that cannot be colonized, that refuse colonization. Anzaldúa used her ethnic and sexual identity to theorize postcolonial hybridity that is both a product of the relationship between colonizer/colonized and a tool which steers us away from the problematic binarisms that have until now framed our notions of culture evoking new ways of being in the world by revisiting the body. Both use visceral knowledge of their in-betweenness in distinct spaces to call for a language to talk about the different, the betweener, the body that challenges colonial and patriarchal constructs. Each of them was engaged in a kind of critical pedagogy that asks for accountability, for knowledges that are situated. Situated knowledges come from the partial, local, incomplete standpoint of the subjugated as a strategy to reposition oneself with greater possibilities of being more, of being part of the humanity in its fullest sense, of being part of a larger family of unrelated Us. We feel like our betweener autoethnographies are carrying these ideas forward, even if we don't know whether any of this will matter for greater social justice one day.

In trying to answer Anzaldúa's call, we write our betweener autoethnographies with the intention of showing our vulnerabilities, exposing our bodies, lives, inner struggles, and shortcomings as they relate to the hostile spaces between Us and Them that we examine. We position ourselves, at times, at the borders of our knowledge in an attempt to create writings from and for the multiple borders and places we have labored and crossed. Both Perez and Anzaldúa have pushed us to take risks in a quest for other ways of knowing, writing, and surviving in a world that seems set in its Us versus Them, dichotomous, hostile, combative ways. They have pushed us to rethink and reinvent our masculinities and ethnicities in ways that have forced us to imagine ourselves as the Other, as those who fight hard to keep hostile ideologies of Us versus Them as the status quo, and in the process contend with our own Us/Themisms in our autoethnographies. The result, we hope, is a form of autoethnography that works to decrease the spaces between academic and non-academic lived experiences, between academics and non-academics, in the space held separate by the hyphen, in spaces between similarities and differences, in the troubled spaces between hope and despair.

Central Metaphor: Betweener Autoethnographies

As Paulo Freire, Frederick Douglass, James Baldwin, and many other thinkers and activists who came before us have posited, there is no path to social justice without reconciliation and healing. Reconciliation lives in the space between Us and Them, and only in reconciliation can we find forms of healing that decrease the distance between Us and Them. Reconciliation searches for similarities of Our human experience in the moments when we feel like outcasts. Reconciliation hopes to transform the hostile spaces between Us and Them into spaces of healing. But before this transformation can take place, *we* need to see ourselves in *them*. *We* need to see *our* own messy, contradictory, self-centered humanity in *them*. We need to take steps to meet the Other halfway between our own notions of Us and Them. And the more entrenched people are into polarizing divisions of Us and Them, the more challenging it is to take the first steps toward the Other with genuine validation, with courageous forgiveness, with a belief that healing the hostile experiences in the spaces between Us versus Them is even a possibility. And we see betweener autoethnographies as a way to tell untold stories and histories that might serve as an initial humanizing encounter with the Other. Our intention with the name *betweener autoethnography* is not the drive to create a new academic concept. Nor is it to differentiate our writing, and ultimately ourselves, from other forms and authors of autoethnography, with the suggestion that ours is a better way of doing autoethnography. We feel that our betweener autoethnographies as a form of qualitative inquiry are not better *than* other forms of autoethnography, but better *with* them. Naming, or creating a name for our writing, comes as a writing process similar to Maxine Greene's description of how artists from the margins come to reimagine public spaces: "Through resistance in the course of their becoming – through naming what stood in their way, through coming together in efforts to overcome – people are likely to find out the kind of selves they are creating" (2000, p. 301).

We hope that betweener autoethnographies help those interested in the search for social justice to become agents for a more inclusive interpretive community, agents in the co-construction of possibilities for reconciliation and healing, co-imagining narratives and relationships where it becomes harder to have a notion of Us *without* and/or *against* Them. Betweener autoethnographies insist that we are all on the same boat, perhaps with each doing our own thing, but with the common bearing toward utopian places of unconditional inclusion, greater social justice, and, ultimately, less suffering and more joy. To us, the appeal of autoethnographies that trouble, interrogate, and engage with the spaces between Us and Them is that all humans experience the joys of belonging *and* the distress and sadness of being excluded. Even the most privileged amongst us experience being treated poorly and put in hostile categories of Them, of the undesirable Other, at some point in life. As we have written elsewhere (Diversi & Moreira, 2009), we recognize that we don't all suffer the same way, that centuries of brutal colonizing ideologies and practices continue to take an oppressive toll much greater on indigenous, female, LGBTQ+, and colored bodies. We recognize the ever present power differentials in systems of exclusion, oppression, and dominance. And examining and troubling these power differentials shaping and informing current imaginations of Us versus Them, of White supremacy, of Western supremacy, of heteronormal supremacy, of male supremacy, of class supremacy, of colonial settler supremacy, and all the ways humans continue to systemically exercise dominance over one another, over fixed categories of the Other, is the critical element of betweener autoethnographies as a method of qualitative inquiry. Examining and troubling ideologies of domination that can only exist when people accept Us versus Them as inevitable, unavoidable, normal, intractable, is at the core of between autoethnography as a critical way of knowing, as a decolonizing form of inquiry, as a humanist epistemology. At the same time, ontologically, we see our communality in the experience of being treated as *lesser humans* as an opportunity to get to know each other with enough depth to eventually see glimpses of ourselves in the Other, as an opportunity to "feel" the Other as part of ourselves. All humans share the experience of being treated as the Other as we journey through life. And it is in this common human experience of being Them that we see betweener autoethnography as a possibility for qualitative inquiry to continue toward imaginations of social justice.

In the next chapters, in Part II, we share betweener autoethnographies that we have co-written since our first book about being and doing scholarship as betweeners searching to expand the circle of Us. In these texts, we insert our betweener bodies in history in order to find our way toward social justice now and in the future. James Baldwin reminds us with words that still echo in the present, with the same urgency of his time: "If history were past, history wouldn't matter. History is the present… you and I are history. We carry our history. We act our history" (Baldwin & Mead, 1974, p. 25). We hope readers also find betweener autoethnographies a form of qualitative inquiry, while at the same time an ontological and epistemological way of knowing about erasing the distance between Us and Them, to be a meaningful path toward social justice.

PART II
Betweener Autoethnographies

3

BETWEENNESS IN WRITING AND PERFORMATIVITY

Betweeners Speak Up

> We write together, and we refuse to be forced into the positivistic reductionism that creates an illusion of order and rank in a collaboration marked by love, respect, and admiration for one another. So we tossed a coin in the air.

Beginnings

We have written a book and several articles together in the past few years and the coin toss is how the order in authorship has been decided. The coin toss is, of course, a simple metaphor for our attempt at subverting the hierarchical legacy of logical positivism. We cannot imagine a way to measure the amount of contribution each of us has had in our collaborative writing. Frankly, this hierarchical logical-positivist structure does not make sense to us. It goes against our deepest ontological and epistemological stances. We write from a Paulo Freirean (1970, 1995/2004, 1998a, 1998b) notion that conscientização can only emerge from people coming together in respectful dialogue with the common goal of liberation from oppressive systems.

We don't know which came first, our reading of Paulo Freire or our friendship, but combined, conscientization and friendship have taken us to intellectual imaginations we could not have reached on our own. From our first collaborative writing experience, we couldn't tell, most of the time, who came up with the ideas for titles, themes, angles, styles, tone, words. But even in the few instances where we could tell, we knew it was all entrenched in a friendship that started on a sunny day back when we were in our late teens, in the casual ease of youth determined to live well against the impossibilities in front of us.

Even then we knew we were crossing thick borders of class in a country, Brazil, marked by 500 years of nearly impermeable stratification. Unless one was born in a berço dourado, a golden crib, higher education was the necessary path in social mobility. And this path was, and continues to be, very narrow for the vast majority of Brazilian youth. The top universities in Brazil are sponsored in full by state and federal governments, and thus are free to students who get in through a competitive national examination. The stinging irony is that students from the public system rarely get an education with enough quality to compete for a spot – in order to get into a free university one needs to be able to afford many years of private schooling.

We, the authors, came from the opposite ends of this class spectrum. When we met, Marcelo was attending his first year in a free university without having to work to pay the bills or have play-money. Claudio was done with high school and already working to support himself and help out his family. That was 25 years ago and we have talked about how we knew right then about these parallel worlds. We shared frustration and anger toward a system rigged to privilege a few at the expense of the large majority. Perhaps it was this common feeling of injustice that allowed us to develop a deep friendship and affection for each other through the bifurcation in our paths in those early years.

We found common ground in music that spoke of border crossers, with characters and storylines that struggled to smuggle themselves into better lives.

We lived our separate lives by day but came together in poetry and revolutionary longing by night.

When the time came to write together, we knew that we could learn from each other's class-based visceral experience of injustice.

Through our border-crossing friendship, we caught glimpses into each other's class with the empathy of Freirean brothers.

Marcelo learned from Claudio what going hungry amid great wealth can do to a young soul.

Claudio learned from Marcelo that a rich person could really care about issues of social justice.

Marcelo saw the subtle discrimination Claudio encountered in the social life of young people. My well-to-do friends didn't say hello to him when I wasn't present.

Claudio saw in Marcelo someone who understands his pain and respects his view of the world. Never pity or a romanticized reality... Marcelo never asked me why I was/am so angry!

Marcelo realized, early on in our friendship, that he would not have gotten to college had he grown up in Claudio's lower social class.

Claudio wondered what it would be like to grow up in a social class where college is a taken-for-granted step toward adulthood. Moreover, what it would be to have a car, a motorcycle, at such an early age.

We couldn't become each other. But we got closer to understanding each other's class trappings, privileges, and burdens than any sociology theory could at the time.

We realized that we could write for a decolonizing way of knowing, for a sociological utopia where visceral experience of oppression could count at least as much as theoretical analysis spun from unearned privilege.

It was an ambitious proposition. But one that seemed possible because of our border-crossing friendship and caring collaboration. Writing together feels like the completion of many intersecting experiences in our lives: friendship, global migration, profession, scholarship, knowledge production, and a hopeful (delusional?) vision of unconditional inclusiveness.

Writing Visceral Knowledge in Decolonizing Times

Writing together gives us an epistemological entrance in the decolonizing movement. It helps us with another way of returning the gaze to the structural Western system of knowledge production, making it the object of our inquiry.

> difficulty lies in the pressing need for scholars to decolonize and deconstruct those structures [of power] within the Western academy that privilege Western knowledge systems and their epistemologies... The decolonizing project reverses this equation, making Western systems of knowledge the object of inquiry.
> *(Denzin, 2005, p. 936)*

Writing together, we toss away the idea that serious scholars have to produce in
Isolation
In being the all-Western scholar writing in support of an unmarked white middle class academic knowledge construction
Writing in *isolation*
With sometimes beautiful words that still follow
Rules of American market ideology
Where written ideas are *private property*
That refuses to be a part of the decolonizing movement
Even when it claims to understand it
That insists to be in a place
Where gender, class, race are all taken for granted in the very moment that typing fingers fill out the blank fake paper on our computer screens
Always *in isolation*
That insists to be in a place
Where the whole world is at their disposal
For their "right" to research *in isolation*
Where marked bodies are reduced to "data"
That refuses to understand that decolonizing scholarship cannot be produced without having the modes of inquiry at the end of the gaze!
Turning "in" the gaze, the stare, the contemplation, the survey, the observation, the gawk, the scrutiny!

Still
We keep writing together
Between hell and narrative
We research back!
This is Linda Tuhiwai Smith's view on researching back:

> "Researching back," in the same manner of "writing back" or "talking back," that characterizes much of the postcolonial and anticolonial literature... has involved a "knowingness of the colonizer" and a recovery of ourselves, an analysis of colonialism and a struggle for self-determination.
> (Smith, 1999, p. 7)

Our work together is central to our research!
Our lives, bodies, beings that cannot be taken away from our writing
That inhabits the space
Between hell and narrative
But that always rejects *isolation*
Even our single-author pieces are never single-authored. We are always together
With a pointing middle finger
Betweeners speak up
Marcelo is always with me!
Claudio is always with me!
Writing... Performing our viscera... our communities!
Between hell and narrative
Visceral knowledge *always counts*
And so
We write refusing
The illusion that we reach scholarly insights alone
The illusion that we can accomplish ideals of social justice *in isolation*
[Deep breath]
Yet this illusion persists in very concrete ways...
If you don't have sole publications you haven't proven your intellectual worth
If you write with the same person too often, well that's a bit fishy, isn't it?
Who is doing the real work?
A production manager insists, "Who is the leading author?"
"There is no leading author," we say again
"But I need a leading author"
"Why?"
"My software won't let me move to the next page otherwise"
"Okay, so Moreira is the leading author"
"Well, then Moreira's name needs to appear ahead of Diversi's"
"But that is not how the coin toss turned out"
"Excuse me?"

"That is not what our coin said"
"Can I put Moreira in the first-author field? The computer won't let me move to the next page if I don't enter an author in the first-author field."
Shit
[Silent pause with our heads down]

Let's write a book together! Smiles. It came with a sense of surprise. Why didn't we see it before? This possibility right in front of us and our incapacity to see it until that moment... We smile at each other... Writing together... It made a lot of sense to us. At this moment in our narrative, the desire is to say: "Then, the rest is history," while waving our published and award-winning book around in the air.

Yes, our writing empowers us and yet, that was the moment we faced the institutional barriers of the so-called "co-authored" scholarship. We were advised not to write a book together because it would make our scholarship seem weaker in the eyes of our evaluators (i.e., academic colleagues and university administrators). An assistant professor and a post doc should write their own books, period. We needed to justify our book project, to allies and employers alike, from its very beginning.

Since then, there have been so many voices:

> Friendly voice 1: "You need to write your own book! A co-authored one will not help you land a job."
>
> Friendly voice 2: "Congrats on your book! It is a good start. Now, it is time for a serious work, your own single-authored book."
>
> Friendly voice 3: "Be very careful. You have too many co-authored works. Plus, Diversi is the first author of your book."
>
> Friendly voice 4: "Claudio, when preparing for your third-year review, you need to state, very clearly, in the future projects session of your narrative, that your intention is to publish single-author articles."
>
> Friendly voice 5: "Don't even think about writing another co-authored book. It will not help your tenure case at all. Write a more theoretical, down-to-earth, single-author article."

[Deep breath]

But writing together has become imperative to us. How long, we asked each other, will we try to write liberatory texts without questioning the mechanisms of knowledge production in Western academia? How can we borrow Linda Tuhiwai Smith's words for our texts and yet cower before the intellectual property status quo?

How long can we not challenge the academic power structures because of the fear of losing our jobs or not getting one in the first place?

Collaborative writing or bust!

We are not here to name ourselves "Trailblazers" in collaborative writing. We stand on the shoulders of many who came before (Anzaldúa, 1987/1999; Denzin, 2003; Fanon, 1952/2008; Freire, 1970; Lorde, 1984; Madison, 1998).

We are not here to claim that collaborative writing is the only way into the decolonizing project that we are partial to.

Instead, we are here to claim that collaborative writing can help us shift the focus from individual accolades to cooperative and collectivist principles (Moreira & Diversi, 2011).

Knowledge production needs to be connected to a larger view of an empowered social democracy that is fundamentally based on inclusiveness and a greater sense of Us (Diversi & Moreira, 2009).

And we can only reach for it together, in sincere collaboration, with a focus on the divisive problems we face and no regard for individual fame, glory, or promotion.

Writing together is an act of resistance against the academic ranking system and the idea that better work comes from isolated individuals. We are two people, united in friendship, fortunate crossroads, and hope, writing together because it keeps us from worrying about which way the coin will land.

Dismantling the Myth of the Lone Expert

> Dialogue is the encounter between two men, mediated by the world, in order to name the world. Hence, dialogue cannot occur between those who want to name the world and those who do not wish this naming – between those who deny others the right to speak their word and those whose right to speak has been denied them. Those who have been denied their primordial right to speak their word must first reclaim this right and prevent the continuation of this dehumanizing aggression. If it is in speaking their word that people, by naming the world, transform it, dialogue imposes itself as the way by which they achieve significance as human beings. Dialogue is thus an existential necessity.
>
> *(Paulo Freire, 1970, p. 88)*

The lone expert writes alone
often about the borders,
obsessed with the exotic body of the Other,
yet negating the half-breed,
the existence of Betweeners,
of those experiencing life more often *between* clear categories of identity than *inside* them.

Western inquiry has been dominated by the solitary writing of lone rangers of expertise. The lone expert is granted disproportionate narrative space to discourse about the Other, in particular the colonized, the excluded, the oppressed Other. The lone expert is infatuated with the Other in sickly voyeurism. It is sickly because the lone expert standpoint starts from the principle, however conscious, that s/he has an innate right to observe the Other. But, to us, more than anything, the lone expert is infatuated with him and herself. For the lone expert, the exotic Other at the end of the gaze is no more than a *thing* to be interpreted and represented for personal gain, in the form of professional recognition, promotion, ever toward a raking system that resembles neoliberal classism. It is as if the lone expert isn't standing on anyone's shoulders. At the end, the lone expert of the Wicked West sits before a distorted mirror, where he mostly sees his own reflections of the Other.

His mirror is in the order of authorship
His mirror is in the self-congratulatory of sole authorship
Empowered with vanity
Through his God-like eyes (Haraway, 1991)
The lone expert classifies and categorizes
Takes and defines
Violates and exploits
Bodies
Bodies that the lone expert can only see as subjects, participants, informed insiders
But not co-writers
Not co-makers of knowledge

The lone expert writes about the lived experience of dehumanizing systems alone, from a lone theoretical knowledge of the Other, all the while privileging categories of identity and being in the world discovered alone in some individual moment of eureka on a beautifully aged campus. Western inquiry has been dominated by the solitary writing of lone rangers of expertise. This is an old story from an even older world, a world order where the oppressed was denied access to literacy for the purpose of hegemonic storytelling. Think of priests who could tell a single story of God and his nature, desires, dislikes, and punishments. Think of colonial histories told only from the point of view of the conquerors (Grande, 2004; Said, 1978). However, like Anzaldúa, some of us come from different, left-handed, in-between worlds. We inhabit, we are, the Borderlands. We refuse the god's eye and the analytical omnipresence it lends to the lone expert.

By
Be*ing*
Here
Some of us destabilize the vanity of the lone expert
As the sole storyteller of our past together
We are neither the researcher nor the docile subject
By
Be*ing* and wri*ting* together
Here
We move textuality and performativity at once (Conquergood, 1991)
Like Della Pollock urges us to do,
"Exploring alternative modes of scholarly representation" (Pollock, 1998a, p. 44)

Our bodies, Marcelo's and Claudio's, symbolically and concretely creating, "resisting text that goes beyond performativity/textuality to engage an ethic of proximity, an aesthetic of kinesis, and a politic of transformation" (Pollock, 1998a, p. 44).

★★★

We are different bodies coming together onto the empty computer screen, in the *physicality* of the *pretend* paper with different subjectivities, with possibilities to trouble even in a more embodied manner the possibilities of being in and creating new worlds. Writing together, from opposing markers and experiences of social class, we find it inevitable to see and expose the messiness of ways of knowing with our embodied text that escapes, blurs, refuses the page. Trying to become Conquergood, we hug, smile, nod, and lean on each other, thinking: "kinesis: performance as embodied practices of signification." We pose our "writingtogetherbodies" as yet another metaphor and performance of co-constructed meaning-making in opposition to the lone expert and his lone(ly) text. Instead of adopting a view from everywhere, where the lone expert "tells it as it is," we offer a view from our encounter with each other in social class, gender privilege, memories of hunger and despair, oppression and hope. Playing with Della Pollock's words below, we aim to write a *human thing* that

> not only privileges performance [*collaborative writing*] but, in doing so, also [*challenges*] the spatial(ized) hierarchy that has so long disenfranchised it [*collaborative writing*]. The oppositional structures [*of either expert or subject of knowledge production*], on which the hierarchy depends, work for text [*the lone expert*]. But reversed, the hierarchy will not hold. It is overwhelmed by sensuality, activity, play, desire, affect, and (shape-shifting) agencies.
>
> *(Pollock, 1998a, p. 40)*

Writing together is a duet that can enrich and expand and deepen the reverberations of the text. It can go beyond the claim that life is messy by *showing* the ever fleeting nature of categories of the Other performed in textual representations. In the encounter of two authors coming from opposing social classes in Brazil, suddenly the representation of being Brazilian, an immigrant category of Other in the United States, is forced to contend with divergent visceral experiences of oppression: one from the position of the oppressed, one from the position of the privileged – yet both united by *conscientização* (Freire, 1970) and by a decolonizing imagination (Diversi & Moreira, 2009; Moreira & Diversi, 2010; Moreira & Diversi, 2011).

Together, we return the gaze of competitive ways of knowing back onto itself. The lone expert regurgitates in writing nothing but the projections of his lonely and distorted mirror (to be sure, the lone expert can be feminine, but "its" gender cannot yet escape the patriarchal overtures of Western ways of knowing). Writing together, we are no longer lonely. And our distortions take on more bearable, more meaningful shapes. There is no first author in our *human thing*. We write together, and we refuse to be forced into the positivistic reductionism that creates an illusion of order and rank in a collaboration marked by love, respect, and admiration for one another. So, once again, confronted with a politics of knowledge production that insists on measuring our value as scholars by the rank in our authorship,

We toss a coin in the air
The coin lands and it's tails
And we are both happy that the coin seems to know who needs it the most today
Collaborative writing or bust!
The coin will continue to fly

Structural Power and Its Epistemological Gatekeepers

Thinking and debating about the tensions and inconsistencies of representing the Other from the lone expert standpoint, Bryant K. Alexander's words on the tricky grounds of racial encounters come back to us:

> the new cultural member or the body trapped in a moment of encounter; the vulnerability of the racial critique – placed in a probationary standpoint or status until some decision of membership is determined; a trail, provisional experimental or luminal stage of racial and cultural assessment that challenges authenticity while reflexively turning attention to an unstable set of criteria that exists only in the collective of a communal thought.
> *(Alexander, 2012, p. 100)*

Betweener bodies are always trapped in the moment of their encounter with the hegemonic binary system of knowing in Western knowledge production. The assumption, incorrect (Rorty, 1999), is that the world is composed of *made* and *found* things, and that serious and respectable knowledge is produced when reality is found, uncovered, interpreted, and represented by the lone expert. Thus the persistent power of binary systems of gatekeeping in academia: Male or female? Rich or poor? Old or young? Homosexual or heterosexual? Informed participant or outlier? Data or noise? Science or fiction? Verbatim or recalled? Objective or subjective? Book or journal article? Real or imagined? Made or found? Expert or subject? Mentor or student? Leader or led?

It does not matter how many times we write, as we did in our first collaborative writing project, *Betweener Talk*: "We can't press the keys at the same time. But this introduction and the entire book are ours. Equally ours" (2009, p. 13). It doesn't seem to matter how many times and how many different ways we try to get our voice across the academic walls, academic gatekeepers return with the same question, over and over again: But who is the first author?

No, really!
Who *is* the first author?
We toss coins in the air to see whose name appears first on the author line
And the deans ask,
But who is *the* first author?
We start articles by stating that there is no first author here
And the chairs ask,
But who is the *first* author?
Goddamn it, there is *no* first author!
Okay, but Claudio, your name appears second in the book, not first
Goddamn it, there is *no first author*!
Fine, Marcelo, fine. What is your co-author's *last name*?
Moreira
Phew! At least your *name will appear first*, says the lone expert gatekeeper.

★★★

Yet, writing together is what we do. Unlike what the coin tells us, from the probationary standpoint we inhabit Claudio will always be the second author of our first book. This is a frequent and concrete response of our institutions to our collaborative work. We don't want to lose our jobs, but we believe that writing together we perform resistance toward the lone expert system, a system that continues to privilege high theory over the visceral experience of being the Other (Diversi & Moreira, 2009). We believe that through performativity writing "the hierarchy will not hold" (Pollock, 1998a, p. 40). We both have conversations with our chairs, deans, and provosts to have our writing accepted with the same weight and respect as the lone expert's. As much as. No more. No less.

Writing together gives us more insights about systems of oppression and subjugation of the Other than writing alone. We bring our own solo ideas to the start of our writing projects and, before too long, we get inspired, challenged, and ultimately transformed by each other. We bring the classic and not-so-classic texts of our distinct disciplines and, united by a shared decolonizing praxis, make interdisciplinary connections that wouldn't be possible if we were writing alone. We introduce each other to new authors, books, articles, colleagues, and in the process increase our library of knowledge beyond the limitations of our own intellectual horizons. When one gets stuck in the inevitable writer's block vortex, the other picks up the text and moves it along to a place where the block crumbles away. And on the rare occasion when we both get stuck, on a concept or on the arc of the story we are trying to tell, the anxiety is assuaged by the camaraderie and a deep sense of trust in each other. Together, it feels more possible to believe we will find a way out of writing predicaments.

Writing together from different disciplines and social classes allows us to reach intellectual and emotional places that were impossible for us alone. The lone expert cannot reach, much less inhabit, this space. The lone expert and producer of knowledge cannot see, much less understand, the Other's lives in this space of betweenness:

> The white man is always trying to know into somebody else's business. All right, I'll set something outside the door of my mind for him to play with and handle. He can read my writing but he sho' can't read my mind. I'll put this play toy in his hand, and he will seize it and go away. Then I'll say my say and sing my song.
>
> *(Zora Neal Hurston, 1935/1990, p. 3)*

The lone expert cannot conquest Emma Perez's "decolonial imaginary" (1999), mainly because he can't quite 'see' that the "decolonizing project reverses this equation, making Western systems of knowledge the object of inquiry" (Denzin, 2005, p. 936). Isolated ways of knowing that are more concerned with individual credit, certainty, and theoretical supremacy perpetuate ways of knowing that persist in excluding the non-expert from representation and knowledge production. Ranking of authorship is but one structural and institutional way the Other has been excluded from the making of knowledge production, even as s/he continues to be the object of study of the benevolent, privileged, and lone expert.

But it does not need to be so. This is not an either/or proposition where collaborative writing overturns the table and becomes the dominant way of writing scholarship. It's instead a both/and proposition, where collaborative writing should be included as a legitimate way of knowing about the Other. From our "writingtogetherbodies," we look for narratives that make healing from our "social ills" possible (Spry, 2011). Together, we look for a "writing that saves lives" (Clough, 1994, p. 6), in particular lives lived in-between categories of identity, between Us and Them, between hurt and pissed off.

For nobody can heal alone
Not even the lone expert
As we learned from Paulo Freire (1970)
Only the oppressed can liberate the oppressor
"Despite our desperate, eternal attempt to separate, contain, and mend, categories always leak" (Minh-ha, 1989, p. 94)
There, between oppressors and oppressed
Resides us, betweeners, blurred bodies
Borders and
Writing
Because together, and only together we are

We write
Beyond the border between colonization and
The decolonizing utopia (Diversi & Moreira, 2012)
We, as border smugglers, through our collaborative writing, bring back to the ivory tower,
Possibilities
Bodies
Viscera
Writing and resistance
Together

 Again, inspired by Della Pollock's words: "The oppositional structures, on which the hierarchy depends, work for text. But reversed, the hierarchy will not hold. It is overwhelmed by sensuality, activity, play, desire, affect, and (shape-shifting) agencies" (Pollock, 1998a, p. 40).
 Shape-shifting betweeners, we perform community, resist individualistic isolation "no one can say a true word alone – nor can she say it for another, in a prescriptive act that which robs others of their words" (Freire, 1995/2004, p. 88)
 We keep writing and tossing the coin in the air
 We want to end where, around 2007, we started our first project

> Even as I type this sentence, 2,000 miles away from my writing partner, I know that these words, meanings, intentions, and emotions reside not in me but in us. Most of what we have written... inhabits the memories of our conversations, discussions, and occasional disagreements. We already do not remember who first brought up a significant number of ideas and concepts central to this [text]. And after a few attempts at keeping the story straight, we gave in and embraced the exhilarating experience of truly co-constructing a [text] together. We have found a dialogic voice that has made our individual work more meaningful, grounded, and, yes, fulfilling. We have found a voice we did not have in our work alone, a voice that seems, to both of us, more vibrant, truer to our experiences as betweeners and decolonizing scholars. Indeed, because of our collaboration in every line of this book, we feel we have achieved a higher understanding of what it means to be a betweener and a postcolonial scholar.
> (Diversi & Moreira, 2009, p. 13)

4

BETWEENNESS IN SYSTEMIC EXCLUSION

When Janitors Dare to Become Scholars

The colonizers spent centuries trying to impose their language. The colonized people were told either verbally or through message systems inherent in the colonial structure that they did not possess effective cultural instruments with which to express themselves. This language profile imposed by the colonizers eventually convinced the people that their language was in fact a corrupt and inferior system unworthy of true educational status (Freire & Macedo, 1987, p. 118)

"I still think the communicative burden is on you to improve your English," Marcelo says, teasing but serious.

"I agree," says Claudio, "but the burden is also on the native speaker to try and understand my broken English. I am Claudio. I have a pony-tail, sometimes a beard, and always a few earrings. I love my partner, daughter, and son. My English may not be perfect, but nobody can tell my experiences of oppression as well as I can."

"I think I understand your position on this a bit better. Are you saying that much of the criticism toward your broken English and lack of theoretical sophistication is still informed by the colonialist legacy present in higher education?" Marcelo asks.

"Yes, that is the point I want to elaborate on here," Claudio says. "And it's not a self-pity party. I think this unspoken elitism continues to shape the dominant discourse on what constitutes scholarly work in the U.S."

"Alright. I agree. Even many self-proclaimed postcolonial scholars privilege detached analysis of lived experience over visceral knowledge, where the very humans suffering oppression are deemed, by self-appointed intellectual superiors, too emotional and atheoretical to be logical and sensible," Marcelo says.

"And it goes beyond that, in my view," Claudio says jumping in, "the very people who are treated with renewed dignity in the writings of well-meaning, conscientious academics are denied entry in the production of knowledge coming out of elite universities."

"But not overtly so, of course," Marcelo says probing.

"No, not overtly so, at least in my experience, which makes this form of modern colonization even harder to challenge in the public discourse. This colonization continues to keep the oppressed out of mainstream knowledge production via micro details of the graduate school experience, that is, structure and language."

"Give me examples," Marcelo interrupts.

"I want to focus on language here, but I can mention a few structural problems that continue to keep us, exotic subjects, out of academic knowledge production. Graduate students are often discouraged from keeping jobs outside of school, for instance. But what graduate program can truly support a graduate student candidate with a family to care for, or someone without social capital and thus without the help of parents, companies, or even credit cards. A person without an address may not be allowed inside a bank, let alone qualify for a student loan. Then there is the issue of work-load expectations. Programs and profs dish out course and research work like students have nothing else to do but graduate school. The list goes on, mate. I know it. I barely survived the roadblocks in my own progressive graduate programs. But I want to come back to language as the focus of this textual performance." Claudio catches his breath.

"So what about language as a colonizing factor in knowledge production?" Marcelo asks after a brief silence.

"It's a delicate thing to discuss, especially for someone with Bad English like me," Claudio says in jest.

"Because people think you are whining," Marcelo adds.

"Or because people think I have a chip on my shoulder, or that the world is out to get me, or some other conversation turn off," Claudio says.

"So, do you?" Marcelo asks.

"What?" Claudio says, his tone a bit sharp.

"Have a chip on your shoulder?"

Claudio's lips tighten a little. "Of course I do! THAT is the point! And the chip is on my shoulder not only because I have experienced undue hardship but because I am told I can't write about my experiences until I can use language like the privileged! The chip gets extra heavy when that happens. And I know mine is NOT a unique experience in academia. And I want to give language to this hidden colonialist barrier, to name it, to expose it, so we can then overcome yet another invisible mechanism of oppression. Though I can only do it using my Bad English," says Claudio, openly appreciating the irony.

"Let's start with your recent rejection then," Marcelo suggests.

I was born in Brazil, the famous mestiço country known for its samba, soccer, and injustice.

I do not dance

I do performance but am not an actor
English is not my mother tongue
Troubling
And
Troubled by
My Bad English
I would like to tell you a tale...

"Some time ago, I submitted a manuscript to a top-tier academic journal in the field of communications. The paper was called *My Bad English: A Letter to Norman Denzin*. The paper was rejected," Claudio starts.

"Everyone gets manuscripts rejected," Marcelo says, "why do you think this rejection reflects academic snobbery toward your language skills?"

"My intention here is not to put myself above criticism. I even liked some of the critical comments. I am using this experience here not to talk back to the reviewers about the paper. My intention is to use some of the comments to address issues of the visceral knowledge I have tried to develop in my work and life, hopefully allowing us to move towards a practice of inclusive social justice inside academic walls: an exercise in decolonizing inquiry and the academy. Two review comments made me uneasy...

1) To me, it looks like some personal anecdotes with a few scholarly quotes thrown in to give it a bit of a scholarly cachet.

2) And, yes, I am now deploying the rules of a writing system that privileges certain ways of speaking. I would argue that there are some good reasons for holding to those conventional norms. Most often those norms are guided by the desire for communicative clarity.

In my opinion, *My Bad English* shows how alternative forms of discourse offer alternative insights. Such alternative insights ARE in the story. What is being called anecdotes I call, as I learned from Haraway (1991), people's lives. To dismiss lived experience as 'anecdote' makes no sense to me. This shows not only ignorance but also intolerance and arrogance of the academic world," Claudio says.

"The ones who know best," Marcelo agrees.

"Like Freire says,"

> It's impossible to talk of respect or dignity that is in the process of coming to be, for identities that are in the process of construction, without taking in consideration the conditions in which they are living and the importance of the knowledge derived from the experience, which they bring to school. I can in no way underestimate such knowledge. *Or what is worse, ridicule it.*
> (Freire, 1998a, p. 62, italics added)

In the end it goes back to who has the power to (mis)read the Other.
Am I a fake? The false scholar?
No

I am
The personal anecdote
The quote
The scholarly cachet
All at the same time
In my hybrid body
I pass when I talk right
But am I a pretentious anecdote when I say
Foucault doesn't know my oppression
Better than me?

"A postcolonial concept of class is there, in the *My Bad English* story, and it seems to me that it makes people uncomfortable or simply goes over their heads. It is a matter of writing against the VERY form of ACADEMIC writing, not for the sake of anarchy or nihilism but for the sake of egalitarian inclusion of those less academically sophisticated. More than a syntax issue, it's a class issue that is still being ignored, wittingly and not, in higher learning.

To exclude ways of knowing for the sake of rules forming a writing system, for the sake of communicative clarity, clarity to those who haven't lived oppression in visceral ways, is not for me."

"Not to mention it won't help advance the decolonizing project," interrupts Marcelo.

"I position myself against these excluding rules of scholarly language. I position myself against the either/or dichotomy of proper language use in academia. I want something more inclusive, as in both effort toward clarity and effort to understand those with Bad English. It is not about transforming, training, and educating the oppressed/colonized Other into some privileged model."

We pause to think. Paulo Freire comes to mind again.

"The more you have freedom to criticize, the more necessary is the sacredness of the domesticating social order for its self-preservation. In this sense, schooling at whatever level plays one of the most vital roles, as an efficient mechanism for social control. It is not hard to find educators whose idea of education is '"to adapt the learner to his environment," and as a rule formal education has not been doing much more than this (Freire, 1985, p. 116)."

We agree. It is about a dialogue that honors what this person knows and what she/he brings to table; the visceral knowledge; and what she/he and his/her community identify as their problem. Good ol' Paulo Freire.

Claudio continues.

"I was a janitor and a grad student. Now I am a semi-illiterate in two languages that holds a Ph.D. Now, deal with me... try keeping me out."

"Nobody is trying to keep you out now," Marcelo says.

"Maybe. I am new at this, at being a regular faculty member. But up to me taking this job, struggling against a system that tried to keep me out was part of my daily life. I don't want to dwell in the past. But the past isn't that far back.

And the scars of the past don't disappear just because things are good now," says Claudio.

"That is a key point," Marcelo agrees.

"Of course I am not the first to make this point. Think of Gloria Anzaldúa's class struggle, or bell hooks' (1981) cry: 'Ain't I a woman?' Again, the list goes on. But let me get back to the rejected paper and the reviewers' language comments. Here Reviewer 2 demands communicative clarity":

> And, yes, I am now deploying the rules of a writing system that privileges certain ways of speaking. I would argue that there are some good reasons for holding to those conventional norms. Most often those norms are guided by the desire for communicative clarity.

"That makes me think of yet another quote from Freire," Marcelo says.

> For us progressive educators, it does not matter if we teach biology, the social sciences or the national standard language, it is fundamental that we respect the cultural identity that passes through social classes of students. It is necessary to respect students' language, its syntax and its semantics. It is this respect that is not present when we disregard or minimally regard the discourse of children from subordinate classes. Particularly when we more than insinuate and make our dislike obvious for the way those children speak, the way they write, the way they think, by labeling their speech inferior, and incorrect. It is precisely this that takes place in the so-called multicultural societies where language and hegemonic cultures smash and belittle the language and culture of so-called minorities.
>
> *(Freire, 1970, pp. 134–5)*

"Clarity? For whom?" Claudio asks.

"For all," says Marcelo. "Claudio, there is the necessity of being culturally bilingual. We need to be able to speak with and be understood by the street child and the intellectual."

"Remember that I, my body, my English... got here from the streets. Perhaps you can be culturally bilingual. I am working on it. But I am not yet. It might be, as I suggest, that we are still silencing the less educated with our hegemonic ways of producing scholarship," Claudio says.

Or
It may be that
I am a fake
Scholar
Person
A human almost being or
A being almost human

"My point is: What happens to the one who is not able to be bilingual? Who will be left out of the university walls? Or are we to be satisfied with a system that privileges grad students that are young and single? I don't think so.

Should I apologize for being married and having two children while I was a grad student? For not having enough time for books? You know, those damned Latinos are always pregnant. We might be pregnant again right now writing these words."

"I hope not, as another pregnancy would jeopardize your tenure," Marcelo taunts.

"Exactly!" says Claudio, the janitor-scholar.

Claudio goes on.

"Returning to what happens to the one that is not able to be culturally bilingual: Perhaps I am not able to be one. The so-called academic clarity is confusing to me. The way I learn, read, and write does not fit in these rules. They don't make sense to me. I am not able to be articulate and so should I be quiet?"

"Hardly, amigo, but if you shout at people who are trying to listen to you, then you undermine the very dialogue you are trying to promote," says Marcelo.

"Okay, perhaps I do come across as being angry at the world sometimes. But if you haven't encountered the mundane everyday discrimination I have, and many Others have, then you have no visceral experience of the overwhelming frustration and sense of injustice we feel in mainstream academia," says the janitor-scholar.

"So perhaps this point is what needs to be made clearer."

"It IS hard to exist in this place in-between," Claudio says interrupting, "the transition from janitor to scholar, from a poor homeless Brazilian kid to a producer of knowledge about the oppressed Other, hits so many status quo walls that we sometimes have to shout in anger to be heard."

"Yes, yes, power has to be taken and not given, etc. I understand that in my own epistemological-betweener way. But I also think we can't decolonize knowledge production by shouting only. We need to get better at engaging the dominant politics of knowledge production in Rorty's (1979) notion of endless search for consensus, not Truth," Marcelo chimes in, suddenly aware of his name dropping.

Claudio nods and smiles at the slip.

"Inspired by Anzaldúa, what I've been doing is asking to be met halfway. During my academic years, I've been in a friendly yet intense discussion with a mentor and friend, Professor Dan Cook. It impressed me how much I wrote to answer his challenging questions. In the end, there is a significant point where Cook and I disagree. Cook believes that there is an important kind of knowledge that comes from the university that allows us to interpret and analyze the lives of others, which somehow is essential to a scholar. I don't. I believe that there is an important body of knowledge that is important for survival in oppressed conditions that is as essential as the other is, and there should be space for it in the university besides the 'subject's point of view' as told by the learned scholar. I want to be the translator and decoder for me, for my bunch. Here is another no-no. I want to quote our own words here," Claudio says.

"Don't do that," Marcelo adds quickly, "it's not scholarly to quote yourself."

We both enjoy the mixture of dialectical tension and self-deprecating humor. We are both betweeners pushing for more narrative space for decolonizing knowledge production in academia, we are both Brazilians and male, both scholars in American universities. Similarities abound in age, accent, and multicultural experiences. Yet, we come from drastically different social classes and, thus, different formal education and language socialization paths. Marcelo wants to follow some established scholarly traditions for the sake of interdisciplinary dialogue. Claudio wants to do away with established scholarly traditions exactly for the same reason. Marcelo doesn't want to quote ourselves. Claudio does. But we agree that dialogical transparency is an essential aspect of decolonizing knowledge production. So here is what Claudio thinks we said best elsewhere:

> This is our way of looking, examining, reflecting, interpreting, and representing life at the margins of society. We are not claiming this is the only or best way of writing social sciences about and against the ideologies of domination that underlie the stories of us-versus-them we bring together in this book. We are claiming, however, that visceral knowledge has been kept at bay (when not completely denied) in the social sciences in the English-speaking world. We are claiming that the dominant discourse in academia is still colonized by the ontological dualism of logical-positivism (i.e., idealism versus materialism, mind versus body, fact versus fiction, science versus arts). In both of our experiences as young scholars, we have witnessed an endless string of self-proclaimed resistance scholars declaring to value lived experience while, under the same breath, continuing to privilege theory over practice, Foucaultian analysis of power over pedestrian narratives of blood and profanity. We are here to spread our wings and add to the visceral knowledge on oppression we see as scarce in the social sciences in general and the critical postcolonial inquiry in particular.
>
> *(Diversi & Moreira, 2009, pp. 12–13)*

The janitor-scholar goes on.

"At the beginning of my academic life in the States, I felt lost. Many of my writings came with comments such as, 'It's not a sentence,' or 'I do not believe you have the skills, English and otherwise, to succeed here.' Oh, the difficulty of reading and writing theory, small tasks that my classmates seemed to take for granted and move on. I felt dumb. I am not smart enough. Stop pretending... who was I trying to fool? This may look like a report that a social scientist would write about many high school drop-outs."

"True that, amigo!" Marcelo agrees.

"Most of the classes I took did not speak to me. The fact that the classes were in a foreign language was not the unexpected problem. The unexpected problem was the foreign representations and interpretations about people like me! I felt desperate. I wanted to give up but Dani and I were pregnant. I did not have a plan B, so I kept on pretending... Analua was born, I started drinking, and as good Latinos, Dani and I got pregnant again," Claudio says, shaking his head.

More Paulo Freire:

> The oppressed suffer from the duality which has established itself in their innermost being. They discover that without freedom they cannot exist authentically. Yet, although they desire authentic resistance, they fear it. They are at one and the same time themselves and the oppressor whose consciousness they have internalized. The conflict lies in the choice of being wholly themselves or being divided; between ejecting the oppressor within or not ejecting him; between human solidarity or alienation; between following prescriptions or having choices; between being spectators or actors, between acting or having the illusion of acting through the action of the oppressors; between speaking out or being silent, castrated in their power to create and re-create, in their power to transform the world.
>
> *(Freire, 1970, pp. 32–3)*

"I am a stubborn person who has a wife and two children and did not have a plan B. I decided to do what I know and do best, to hang in there no matter what, to survive. I stopped drinking. Not drinking, I had a chance.

At the same time, in my 'fieldwork' trips to Brazil I became stronger. The abstract discussions that did not speak to me in the classroom were very far away from the lives I was interacting with in Brazil. Something was wrong and I started to believe it wasn't just me. Jorge Amado's fiction and Chico Buarque's songs have helped me more than the social science writings that I have read and not read. I did not know Foucault or Derrida enough and I did not have the previous formal knowledge, luxury, or privilege/time – we were four people in a foreign country living under a thousand dollars budget – to learn what I did not think I could. But, I knew how to walk in the favelas. I knew how to interact with soccer fans and sugar cane workers. When Justino said to me: 'You know...' I knew it, not with my brain or books, not in a dichotomous fact-fiction way, but with my living body." The janitor-scholar pauses for a moment.

Conscientização,

It was good to realize or remember that we knew stuff.

We started to interrogate the reasons it was so difficult to be in grad school.

The answer was in front of us.

It was for the same reasons it was difficult to make it through high school.

It was the familiar feeling of not belonging, not having friends.

A system that wasn't there for us.

Or did not speak to/for us.

Claudio says, "I did make it through high school and beyond in Brazil, as a troublemaker with weak language skills. Familiar, isn't it?"

"Not so much, really. I don't know of other people with a similar upbringing in Brazil who have gotten this far in the academic world," Marcelo says.

"I mean 'familiar' as in Freire's *Pedagogy of the Oppressed*," clarifies Claudio.

Freire's method for adult literacy is simple yet penetrating. In 1962, Freire's method was able to help teach 300 rural peasants in 45 days in Angico, Rio Grande do Norte, to overcome illiteracy. Living communally with the farmer-workers, a cultural worker was able to identify "generative words" (through sound, size, and cultural meaning) that were important to the workers, words that were part of their everyday life, part of their struggle. Then, always together, workers and teachers would create themes from these words. They would work in the coding/decoding/translation of generative words in discussion sessions known as "cultural circles." Reading and writing the world became a living praxis, the process of conscientização – an ideological struggle and a revolutionary praxis – whereby changing their lives the workers could change the world. Change is possible. History IS possibility.

> We want a truly competent school system: one that respects the ways of being of its students, their class and cultural patterns, their values, their knowledge and their language – a school system that does not assess the intellectual potential of lower-class children with evaluation tools created for those whose class conditions give them an undeniable advantage over the former.
>
> *(Freire 1970, p. 37)*

Freire wasn't referring to higher education. We are.

We are aware of how lucky we are in having an American version of Paulo Freire in our advisor, Norman Denzin. He honors what we know. Norman Denzin (2003) gave us a view of Visweswaran that complicates the notion of an objective, reflexive ethnographer/scholar, and here we quote his interpretation of her words: "She criticizes the reflexive normative ethnographic approach that presumes an observer and a subject with stable identities. She contrasts this stance with a deconstructive ethnography, where the observer refuses to presume a stable identity for self or other" (p. 236). Visweswaran (1994) does not only question the ethnographer/scholar authority. She "forfeits authority."

"And how does she do that?" Marcelo asks, again seeking scholarly clarity.

"In Visweswaran's deconstructive ethnography I can be in the betweener position. I embodied the observer and subject and in doing so, I am messing up with the idea of the ethnographer unifying, through the process of knowledge construction, the relationship between researched and researched that is presented to the reader. Multiple and fragmented possibilities in texts and bodies are possible. Reflexively to question the authority of the ethnographer is not enough. Not anymore; or as Norman Denzin (2003) says 'That is no longer an option' (p. 236). The janitor is here!"

"Who am I? A fake scholar? A Latino male? Dark skin? Light skin? Father, husband, grad student, etc. And I do not want to be the authority in knowledge production about disenfranchised indigenous kids like me. Not in this colonial sense. I wanna be the possibility... Why are language-sophisticated scholars more entitled than I am to produce knowledge about kids like me? Why can't my body, our bodies, be transgressive as a form of scholarship?" Claudio repeats.

"The decolonizing project is just beginning," Marcelo says, nodding in agreement.

"Under the wing of Norman Denzin, with the support and teaching of Dan Cook, Cole, Cameron McCarty, Syndy Sydnor, and my brother Marcelo, I started to identify the 'generative' words in my life, such as knowledge production, theory, method, experience, epistemology, body," Claudio says.

We became the teacher and the student.
We became the cultural worker and the peasant.
We are Anzaldúa's betweener!

Living communally, we traveled back into the past, recollecting forgotten memories, retelling stories that were supposed to be buried, stories not appropriate for telling. We combine these suppressed stories with the lives and places we have lived and labored. We combine these untold stories with the famished/celebrated "fieldwork." We are building our community and reinventing our roots, creating our Freirean version of our cultural circle.

"And I started to write. Not the writing that one should expect from a trained scholar, but the writing that comes from my visceral experience of exclusion as a poor and family-less kid," Claudio says, "the writing that comes from a person who does not formally know enough English, theory, or even Portuguese, my mother tongue, for Christ's sake. It is not only the writing I am able to do, given my skills, but also the writing I want to do."

The writing from the flesh
The writing we believe should be written.
Through this writing, we are able to come back to reading,
The reading that empowers us and not the reading that makes us feel stupid,
Out of place in academia.

"And there is more," Claudio goes on. "Suddenly, I am learning again. I am not in the process of becoming the next White colonized body in academia, though I am far from being the culturally bilingual researcher you speak of."

"So what is your alternative, then?" Marcelo asks.

"I encountered Gloria Anzaldúa's writings and a new world opened up in front of me. She presented a theoretical writing I was able to relate to; a lesbian woman who sold so many books; an icon in Third World feminism; a person who does not quite fit anywhere. In the typical intellectual arrogance of the colonizer, Anzaldúa was not theoretically sophisticated to get accepted as a doctoral student in the History of Consciousness graduate program at the University of California Santa Cruz – the very same program that used her texts to educate its graduate students! Is this, too, another 'anecdote' with a scholarly cachet?"

"Hard to argue against that, I think," Marcelo adds.

"Here is another anecdote close to home," Claudio resumes, "my father is a drunk. Neither my father nor my mother have a college degree, own a house, a car, or have held a regular job in the last 15 years. My sister never went to college and got pregnant when she was 17.

Am I the product of the colonial rape or just the product of a broken family living in a vacuum?

Am I an anecdote?"

And what oppressive anecdote isn't an expression of systemic oppression?" Marcelo says, interrupting again.

"Yes, what happens to the one that is not able to be culturally bilingual? Who will be left out of the university walls?" Claudio says.

"Away from critical knowledge production inside the university!" Marcelo adds.

"Professor Clifford Christians told me about the visit Paulo Freire made at the University of Illinois Urbana-Champaign, Institute of Communications Research, in the 1970s. At the end of his speech, looking around the audience made up of students and faculty, Freire asked: 'Where are the workers?'"

"Not invited as knowledge construction participants, of course," Marcelo pipes in. "Similarly, Jones (1997), in her powerful performance, 'Sista Docta: Performance as Critique of the Academy,' asks the academic audience: 'Where are the sista doctas?'" the janitor-scholar pushes on.

Where are the workers?

Where are the sista doctas?

Where are the fellow humans we call oppressed, marginal, disenfranchised?

They appear in scholarly texts but aren't invited to promotion parties.

They are used in the production of knowledge – and to clean bathrooms, serve in cafeterias, and operate lawn mowers – that takes place inside the Ivory Tower.

But they are too uncouth for the faculty room,

Lecture halls,

Journals.

"Speaking of journals and the language of knowledge production..." Marcelo prompts Claudio.

"Right. Here is another comment, this time from Reviewer 1, who was mostly supportive of my manuscript," Claudio says.

"It isn't enough to simply suggest that one's background is responsible for the language one uses – what does a particular language usage reveal?" writes Reviewer 1.

This is a question for you, too.

We have felt isolated in school because our world isn't represented in them.
We are in unfamiliar surroundings that claim to speak on our behalf,
The downtrodden.
The learning processes for survival in the streets is craftiness,
And in scholarship it's The Method,
The one supposed to reveal the Truth behind oppression.
Well, it doesn't!
Indeed, it dismisses their own sanctified notion of Truth
By calling it anecdote.

"Alright, are you presenting an either/or solution here?" asks Marcelo, "are you saying we should do away with theory about oppression?"

"I am not denying the importance of abstract works in academia. They are important in the advancement of the cause of an inclusive social justice, as analytical tools, as a power counter-punch to dogma, etc. What I am saying here, again, is that there are people much better prepared and willing to do that kind of work.

Folks like me, without an educated upbringing, enter the decolonizing dialogue through lived experience. I write 'some personal anecdotes with a few scholarly quotes thrown in to give it a bit of a scholarly cachet," quips Claudio, "and I do so for the sake of clarity to those who, like me, are interested in participating in the postcolonial movement in academia not only as subjects of research but also as producers of knowledge."

We can tell this story and break the silence
The silence that privileges the abuser
A silence that is essential to systems of oppression
We can tell this story and break the silence
The disguise of equality
Itself buried under layers of theory
And standards of communicative clarity
We've been called many names
However, it is our task to name ourselves
We call ourselves teachers and educators
Because we love
Conscientização

Shortly before his death, Freire was reported as saying something to the effect that he "could never think of education without love and that is why I think I am an educator, first of all because I feel love" (McLaren, 2002, p. 253).

"It seems to me," Claudio says, "that even the quotes I choose do not quite sound very scholarly."

"That is why it's good to cite McLaren citing Freire, to give it the scholarly cachet of authority," adds Marcelo.

"Even though I am scared, my intention is to hang in there no matter what," Claudio says. "And I take inspiration from these specific words from Freire, at the end of his life."

> When we are faced with concrete fears, such as that of losing our jobs or not being promoted, we feel the need to set certain limits to our fear. Before anything else, we begin to recognize that fear is a manifestation of being alive. I do not hide my fears. But I must not allow my fears to immobilize me. Instead, I must control them, for it is in the very exercise of this control that my necessary courage is shared.
>
> *(Freire, 1998b, p. 41)*

"Yes, I am hanging in there no matter what," the janitor-scholar goes on, "and the only way to keep me from pointing out the masked disdain for the embodied oppressed in academia, to this very day, is to take your academic knife and cut my des-articulated, un-theoretical tongue.

But be aware,

I might bite your hand and swallow your fingers... and looking at your fingerless and bloody hand I will go on, crying in my nothingness, making awful utterances in my tongueless mouth, drinking coffee

And

Smoking cigarettes."

"But this is never going to happen, is it?" Marcelo asks rhetorically, "as we, academics, tend to work only in abstraction."

"Unless someone, high above, using the rights of the Patriot Act, decides that I have not behaved well, that I am a threat to the only real democracy in the world, and silences my accented tongue... and this time for good," Claudio says. "Then, you all, 'who know best,' can make good use of your theories and methods, and study, classify, and represent my silenced body.

Because, as I've been told so many times, you have the correct tongue and I don't know theory.

I do not write anecdotes with a few quotes to give it a scholarly cliché. I write about lives and painfully marked bodies!

However, in the end, the truth, as painfully as it is to invoke it here, is simple.

I might be a fake

A poor scholar

But hey, I am a heck of a subject

Am I not?"

"And what do you say to those who claim you are no longer oppressed? You are a college professor in America after all," retorts Marcelo.

"That is where I see the importance of Performance as communicative strategy against the colonizing elitism still shaping and informing academic knowledge production about the Other," Claudio adds quickly. "I contest static notions of oppression/oppressor/oppressed as enforcers of exclusiveness in concepts of the Other. I still live in the betweenness of the postcolonial world: I am privileged in my position of Third World scholar working in a First World institution yet do battle every day against the colonizing paradigms informing education, academic scholarship, and the production of knowledge about the Other."

"Would you clarify what you mean by oppression?" Marcelo asks.

"Here is my answer, or, better, my question: Can one erase the oppression wrought on the marked body?"

"Of course not," agrees Marcelo, "no more than you can look at a scar and say it never hurt because now the pain is gone."

"No more than you can tell a person who went hungry in childhood that he is no longer oppressed. I am the first to acknowledge my privilege. Of course, there are many layers and forms of oppression that come from the intersections of race, class, gender, religion, sexual orientation, and so forth. I've been around misery, violence, and poverty for so long... And I don't dare to compare the good deck of cards that life gave me with many of the lives present in my work. The point I am trying to make here, and what I think is most revealing about academic elitism, is that when this question about oppression is asked, more often than not, it comes from someone who has never been there," says Claudio.

"It's a bit like being European and telling indigenous people not to make a fuss, that colonization is over, happened in the past, they now can vote and are no longer oppressed," Marcelo adds.

"Again, I acknowledge my privilege. But does that voice, when asking this question, acknowledge his? I always go back to the example of Anzaldúa not being accepted as a Ph.D. student at Santa Cruz... Can we erase the oppression in the marked body?

I have a family, a Ph.D., a faculty job at a research institution... However, I remember every violent act I committed, suffered, or witnessed. Remember is not the word I want, it's too soft.

Me, my body and my English... Let me invoke bell hooks: Do not forget the pain. I ain't forgetting it. I can't," Claudio says trailing off in thought.

"Give us another anecdote of oppression from your upbringing," Marcelo asks.

"I remember eating dinner, not sure about tomorrow's meal. Does the fact I am able to eat now erase that? Of course not. Did I know back then, that by just having today's dinner I was much better than many of my childhood friends? You bet I did! You know, this question does not make sense at all. It is a White middle-class question. It is the question I would ask, if I decided to forget... if I decided to be the next White-like scholar... and I ain't the white stuff," replies Claudio.

"Give us another typical question you get, then," asks Marcelo.

"Okay, so because you had a hard life, should we go easy on you? I get that often after I give presentations in conferences. What is really being asked is, since I do not produce good scholarship, am I asking for their lenience and multicultural embrace? No! It's insane... It's the other way around, you see. Where are these questions coming from?"

"Perhaps they come from compassionate conscientiousness," Marcelo says, "but ultimately, folks asking these questions are standing in an ancient pool of unearned privilege."

"Yeah, last time I faced this question, I told the person, Look, I'm here, I need no charity."

"Though you will take it," Marcelo says interrupting.

"If it's convenient, I will. No, seriously, I survived. I'm playing your game on your home turf. I know that if I face adversity I will find a way out. I know I will survive. But let me ask you: What is so threatening about me and the critique about the way even self-proclaimed progressive academics have kept visceral knowledge of oppression under the academic weight of theoretical sophistication?"

"Touché!" Marcelo agrees.

"Paraphrasing Paula Gum Allen: I did more than survive… I loved, had children, nurtured, and went to class. I read, wrote, got published, and taught," says Claudio.

"It's a call to Others who look inside academia and don't see their lived experiences reflected back, at least not in visceral and recognizable ways," Marcelo says.

I hang in there no matter what
Who gives the authority to ask questions?
Who gives the authority to invade people's lives to do research?
Like Anzaldúa, we ask to be met halfway
Then, we can talk
There, in the halfway place,
We can have a dialogue
I beat and got beat
I've been peed on
Lucky me, never peed on nobody
Roni was my friend
Andre was five years old and was raped
In front of a silenced me
The privileged say, you
Are oppressed no more
But can we erase the oppression in the marked body?
Listen to my thick accented tongue
Correct my improper writing
I am a thug with a Ph.D.
We ain't nobody's subject
Do my talk
Sing my song
We cannot erase the oppression in the marked body
But we can allow the wounds to speak up
Through their own

Missing Bodies

To live in the Borderlands means you

> are neither *hispana india negra espanola*
> *ni gabacha, eres mestiza, mulata,* half-breed
> caught in the crossfire between camps
> while carrying all five races on your back
> not knowing which side to turn to, run from;
> ...
> In the Borderlands
> you are the battleground
> where enemies are kin to each other;
> you are at home, a stranger,
> the border disputes have been settled
> the volley of shots have shattered the truce
> you are wounded, lost in action
> dead, fighting back;
> ...
> To survive the Borderlands
> you must live *sin fronteras*
> be a crossroads.
>   *(Anzaldúa, 1987/1999, pp. 194–5)*

Those of us who stand outside the circle of this society's definition of acceptable women; those of us who have been forged in the crucibles of difference – those of us who are poor, who are lesbians, who are black, who are older – know that survival is not an academic skill... For the master's tools will not dismantle the master's house. They will never allow us to bring about genuine change.
        (Lorde, 1984, p. 112)

Like Anzaldúa, Lorde, and many others who came before and after, we also find ourselves at the borderlands of education and outside the circle of what mainstream American academia considers to be acceptable scholarship. And as we will attempt to show in this manuscript, many of our college students and the "street" folks[1] we work with feel similar exclusion and experience unwelcoming borders. Although we come in many flavors, varying idiosyncrasies, and a plurality of cultural backgrounds, we, the authors, believe we all share common lived experiences of visceral exclusion from education in general and higher learning in particular. For many in the academic and activist worlds, the crisis of representation awakened in the 1980s and 1990s in the United States by the first winds of postmodernism coming from European thinkers allowed for the creation of narrative space around issues of authorship positionality and subjectivity, as well as issues about the politics of representation and interpretation. The postcolonial movement has brought in additional – and largely missing – perspectives from Third World epistemologies to the dominant discourse on representing the Other.

Who can speak for whom? Under what power relations? Which bodies continue to determine what constitutes legitimate scholarship? Which bodies continue to be excluded from the making of scholarship?

The missing bodies in contemporary American academia. Here lies the central concern of this paper. We continue to see and experience overwhelming exclusionary practices in education. We are contending here that the very bodies that experience oppression and exclusion first-hand continue to be barred from the higher levels of education in the United States based on colonialist notions (i.e., self-granted power to speak on Others' behalf under the guise of benign paternalism) of expertise and titles. We are not claiming to have a solution or greater insight about the predicament of missing bodies in American academia. Rather, we intend to use our autoethnographic experiences and representations as discussion points about decolonizing ways of knowing and categorizing the Other.

We will use a series of biographical glimpses as instantiations of the persistent colonial landscape we experience in American education, including our experiences in and reading of interpretive communities that claim to represent indigenous and marginalized lived experiences of oppression. We will also use glimpses to illustrate our interaction with the various disciplines shaping and informing our epistemological standpoint and our own decolonizing imaginations for a more inclusive future, education, and beyond. We ask the reader to bear in mind that our citations are not meant to be exhaustive or to be taken as a comprehensive review of the literature and our epistemological and performative positionality (for that, please see Diversi and Moreira). Instead, these theoretical glimpses are meant to give the reader a sense of our readings of critical pedagogy, performance autoethnography, and decolonizing approaches. Finally, we end with a longer glimpse that we hope instantiates both the problem of missing bodies in American academia and our attempt to bring a version of decolonizing performance into our university classrooms.

One more request, if we may: We ask that at the end of each glimpse, if you have the patience, you go back to the starting words by Anzaldúa and Lorde. While we will, throughout the paper, attempt to elaborate on the connections between our biographical glimpses to the historical exclusionary practices Anzaldúa and Lorde underscore, we believe you, the reader, would further resonate with your own biographical, visceral experiences of exclusion in ways we can't fathom from a theoretical standpoint. This, too, is what we ask our students as a way of inviting them to make their own connections between the biographical and historical practices that continue to keep many human kinds (e.g., ethnic minorities, women, Third World and indigenous folk, people with so-called disabilities, LGBTQ and less linguistically sophisticated fellow humans) out of representational practices.

Glimpse 1: The Persistent Case of Missing Bodies in Textbooks

I have not seen her in class this week. I write a quick email asking if everything is alright and click on the send button. Within a few minutes, her reply appears on the corner of my computer screen.

"I am thinking of dropping out…" is all I catch before her message fades away. I stop what I am doing and bring her message to the front of my screen.

"I am thinking of dropping out of all my classes this semester. I need to reevaluate my choice to come here. People have been very friendly, and I am grateful for that. As a Black woman in a White place, I don't take this for granted. But I don't know how much longer I can take this. All the research I read for my classes are about White people, by White people, and for White people. When people like me appear in the textbooks, it's to talk about something deviant, pregnant. Last week, I had to read this textbook chapter for my psychology class about intelligence. It talked about this book, *The Bell Curve*, by some White men from those Ivy League schools out east, about how Black people are not as intelligent as White people. The chapter included some kind of disclaimer about how the science behind the book has been disputed. But it doesn't explain anything about this dispute. It simply goes on to talk about different measures of intelligence. I was so pissed off I couldn't go to class after that. It's nothing new in my education, of course, but this felt like the proverbial last drop. I tried it, I promise. But this place brings me down."

Glimpse 2: Still Separate, Still Unequal

After half a century into the postcolonial movement in Western academia, we find that subjugated bodies continue to be missing from classrooms, faculty meetings, and educational structures everywhere. Where are the excluded bodies? Where is the untheorized visceral experience of everyday discrimination? Despite the demographic changes of the past few decades, the physical presence and point of view of less privileged minorities are largely missing from the landscape of American education. A recent report from the American Council on Education claims that 79 percent of tenured and tenure-track university professors are White, 5 percent Black, 4 percent Latino, 8 percent Asian, and 2 percent other. And this apartheid-like picture is only about ethnicity, of course. The exclusionary practices in American education become an ever more startling antithesis of inclusive democracy when we begin to examine gender, class, sexual orientation, religiosity, cognitive-sensorial-motor abilities, and other categories in our efforts to navigate the politics of identity in the 21st century.

Jones (1997) makes the point about the blatant ethnic gap in American academia with the same sharpness we seek in this manuscript,

> To say that the academy is dominated by white people is an obvious point that misses the more complex reality that white behavior patterns and white thinking dominate the academy. White is at the center of the academy's consciousness, so much so that people who exhibit white behavior patterns do not hesitate to make remarks about welfare and plantations, seemingly oblivious to any racial implications in their remarks.
>
> (p. 58)

Postcolonialism, critical theory, and allied paradigms have long shown us how we got here, to this place of inclusive disembodied discourse. By deconstructing ideologies of domination and technologies of justification, our generation has been able to read narratives criticizing social mechanisms that succeed in making inequality a "normal" byproduct of meritocracy – in the land of opportunity, anyone who dreams big and works hard will be rewarded with a place in the sun; those who don't, well, they need to accept the consequences of their own choices. Or so goes one of the great mythologies of American grand narratives. Critical paradigms may have been articulate at challenging the status quo notion that educational institutions and their inhabitants simply reflect individuals' self-reliance, discipline, race-based intelligence, and work ethic, as if such things could be objectively measured by technologies of justification, as if we all started with the same possibilities for choice, free will, and larger social acceptance. Yet, the everyday visceral experience of an American education is NOT one of diversity, let alone one of inclusiveness on the basic level of being human.

In our Heroes and Holidays ways of "embracing diversity," this visceral experience of *exclusion* often comes coated with good intentions and gentle tones. And though effigies continue to burn across 21st-century America in overt public expressions of hatred toward the Other, exclusionary practices of subjugation tend to happen in more subtle manners than ever before. We experience exclusion in subtexts and performances of uncritical multiculturalism. We get warm invitations to parent-teacher conferences, translated to our foreign languages, but the appointments continue to be unilaterally scheduled for a time that is convenient to the teachers and school personnel. And even when we can make it to these afternoon appointments, we are often confronted by a kindness loaded with assumptions of deficit.

Glimpse 3: The Deficit Subtext

Analua is in first grade already! Time sure flies. Classes started a month and a half ago. Dani and I are having our first meeting with Analua's teacher. Analua loves her teacher and in just ten minutes talking with her teacher, it is clear to us that the teacher cares about Analua. We are so pleased. Then, comes the question.

"Dear Dani," the teacher says turning her head towards my wife, "Are you able to read in English?"

Shock! Analua reads, writes, and speaks English without an accent! It is pretty clear that Dani and I did not get to this country last week... or last year, for Christ's sake.

"Yes," answers Dani.

Then, the white liberal answer, so common, in the white liberal New England: "Good for you!"

Good for us... nice... polite, and cheery... but it NEVER comes with an apology for the assumption that we must be uneducated accented bodies.

"Good for you!"

Really?

Glimpse 4: The Good Intentions that Burn with Reductionism

It's March 2009. We are at our daughter Analua's school. We have a meeting with her teacher. The secretary, who has met us several times before, is coming toward us.

"It is amazing," Dani says to me, in Portuguese, in a lower voice. "Every time I come here this woman has something patronizing to say. I bet she will ask if we want a drink of water using only hand gestures." We smile at each other.

The secretary gets closer and looking at me, not my wife, she says,

"Good morning. Have you written the letter to the principal yet?"

Dani, Analua, and Francisco are going to spend part of the summer in Brazil. Analua is going to miss two weeks of class, so we got instructed to write a letter to the principal, informing him of the trip and the reasons for it.

"Not yet," Dani answers her.

Still looking at me, the secretary continues,

"There is no need to feel embarrassed. You're more than welcome to stop by my office. I am glad to help. The letter to the principal can be very informal, such as..."

Then, this time, getting close to our faces, exaggerating the movements of her mouth, and speaking louder and very slowly,

"TO WHOM IT MAY CONCERN..."

I can tell Dani is about to lose it. She is getting mad. Having volunteered at this very school three times a week for quite a while, Dani had had enough. Still, she made an effort to return the civility.

"We did not write the letter because it is the middle of the semester and Claudio is pretty busy."

"Oh, really?" And looking at me, "Do you attend the community college?"

Glimpse 5: Colonial Assumptions

Someone who looks and sounds like Claudio couldn't possibly, in her well-intentioned yet uncritical mind, be attending one of the four prestigious universities in town, let alone be teaching in one of them. Colonial assumptions... even when the Other's body is present in the highest levels of formal education in America, it tends to be erased by simple gestures of colonial assumptions. At a personal level, we do our best to overlook the colonizing subtexts by focusing on the apparent good intentions of inclusiveness. Good intentions may be an excellent initial step. But without being couched in critical reflection and action, Paulo Freire's praxis, it is simply a more nuanced form of exclusionary social performance.

Glimpse 6: Well-Intentioned Essentializing Assumptions

Possibilities...

The decolonizing performances we both imagine depend on the very possibility of narratives of inclusiveness. But we have been chronically stuck with limited possibilities, as our narratives of inclusiveness continue to be written, in American education, by bodies that don't feel the pain of dismissal on an everyday basis. Such narratives fail to connect us beyond simplistic notions of Us–Them exactly because they continue to be written from disembodied theoretical perspectives. These persistent essentializing assumptions are largely due to an educational system that continues to limit fuller participation of the Other in the process of knowledge production through colonizing representations, where only those with the "right" language, identities, resources, and theoretical libraries can advance through the educational system without justifying their right to be there.

As foreign graduate students in the USA, we experienced great intellectual dissonance between our postcolonial texts, all filled with inspiring messages of unconditional inclusiveness, and the exclusionary practices of educators at all levels of the system we encountered. Many years later, now faculty members in respected higher-learning American institutions, that initial intellectual dissonance has morphed into a mixture of shock, rage, and hope that we can find the strength and imagination to overcome the structural obstacles in expanding this circle of inclusiveness.

To achieve this utopia, we believe we need to advance scholarship and teaching that elevate visceral experience of oppression above sophisticated theories about oppression thought out in the relative comforts of Ivory Tower voyeurism. To be sure, we are not postulating an either/or framework for educational performance acts where theory is replaced by lived experience of oppression. Instead, we are postulating a both/and approach where the bodies marked by systemic exclusionary experiences participate in the composition of the decolonial imaginary (Perez, 1999) as makers of transformative knowledge, not simply as exotic subjects of theory, research, and educational texts – all the while adding missing lived experiences to narratives of possibility about a more inclusive sense of Us.

In the spirit of an outburst of possibilities, we have joined forces, inspired and taught by innumerous critical thinkers who paved the way for our generation, with the central goal of troubling the ubiquitous lack of physical presence of the Other in educational contexts. And we often start our own conversations and teachings with the fundamental question of this manuscript: Where are the missing bodies in American education? Then, we begin to unfold this initial question as far as our stances and imaginations allow. Where are the darker-colored bodies in academia? Where are the hearing- and the vision-impaired bodies? Where are the typically excluded bodies?

Where are the sista doctas?

> Performance reveals the extent to which sista doctas are an absent presence on many U.S. campuses. In performance, the numbers are no longer statistics, but they are specific, distinct women. Performance makes the statistics our experiences as we strain to see who rises when I pose the question. We share the flux of embarrassment, frustration, elation, and anger when the handful of sista doctas come to their feet. In performance, the hypocrisy surrounding the academy's inclusion, and the lunacy of "racial preference" (D'Spuza 1995: 293) granted to African American women is given flesh.
>
> (Jones, 1997, p. 53).

Like Jones, we continue to ask our students, where are the excluded bodies in American education? How long until postcolonial scholars criticizing reductionist knowledge production, particularly untenured ones, stop being harassed under the guise of "scholarship standards" informed and shaped by those who profit the most from uncritical conformity? It may be repetitive, but so are the micro-level mechanisms of exclusion in everyday life. This performative questioning in our classrooms is accusatory, to be sure, but mainly of the system that continues to foster and reward such violent exclusion of bodies and possibilities.

In our reading of the American educational landscape, we see the predicament of missing bodies in academia in dialectical relation with the pervasive siege against methodologies of the heart (Pelias, 2004) by the dominant bean-counting technologies of evaluation. How can we truly promote diversity when even the most promising inclusionary practices of education and sociological imagination continue to be narrated, mostly, by privileged bodies and their privileged identities and standpoints? How can we truly entice minority students to believe in the project of enlightenment through critical thinking when we continue to present pictures of reality through reductionist methodologies and pedagogies, where their bodies and lived experiences are missing, or (mis)represented as exotic, deviant, decontextualized from repeated exclusionary treatment?

No, we are not nihilistic quotas, as a few of our senior faculty colleagues have implied – though they are right about us wanting to rock the boat. While we acknowledge a certain progress toward inclusiveness in the educational landscape, we are all too aware of the sickening dissonance of seeing the Other populate research samples while conspicuously missing from faculty meetings and gate-keeping positions within educational structures, from pre-school to higher education to administration and funding agencies.

We don't know of a single public institution of higher education in the USA that does not include increasing diversity, of students, faculty, and staff, as a guiding and central goal in its strategic plan. However, even sympathetic members of the dominant faculty body can seem at a loss when it comes to identity politics in academia. We are asked to serve in every single committee on diversity on campus. Our images are used to promote our departments and universities beyond the scope of our comfort level. It's an honor to appear on university brochures, billboards, and webpages, we are told. We smile and keep our thoughts to ourselves. We fear the retaliation from those who don't relate, in a visceral way, to our sentiments about being tokenized. We fear the puzzled faces from those who care about our sentiments but who do not understand identity objectification. "Lighten up," we are told with friendly punches on the arm. "Why so angry?" we are asked with smiles. Lest we be accused of having a chip on our shoulders, of being paranoid, we let them exploit our international flavors and darker skins as they present a picture of diversity and inclusiveness nowhere to be found in the daily operations and performances of our institutions.

So what to do?

How do we, educators, scholars, all performers of knowledge and imagination, increase the possibilities of being more than fearful excluders?

Complicated, no doubt.

We realize our decolonizing praxis is limited by our own situatedness and imagination.

But with nowhere else to go, a decolonizing call we make.

And we start with the classroom and the texts we bring into it.

We are teachers and scholars. In our classrooms and betweener narratives we attempt to expose some of the overt and covert mechanisms of exclusion we have encountered in the various educational settings we navigate. We envision the teaching and research process similar to Maxine Greene's (2000) description of how artists from the margins come to reimagine public spaces: "Through resistance in the course of their becoming – through naming what stood in their way, through coming together in efforts to overcome – people are likely to find out the kind of selves they are creating" (p. 231). Relying on this approach and our own experiences, we hope to engage students by casting a call for critical reflexivity and renewed possibilities of inclusion, without attempting to tell them what to think about the Other.

Glimpse 7: Our Bodies in Relation to Performance Studies and Critical Pedagogy

The call to performance in the human disciplines has already been made (Denzin, 2003, 2005, 2009; Alexander, 1999, 2005; Holman Jones, 2005), and so has the pedagogical turn in performance studies (Garoian, 1999; Pineau, 1998; Hill, 1998, to name a few). Much has been written about these schools of thought. Not trying to reinvent the wheel, but to situate our own selves in this ongoing dialogue, we want to show our own understanding of this model.

Garoian (1999), inspired by Freire's pedagogy of hope, suggests that "the resistance to cultural domination represents the performance of [a] political strategy to challenge the body politic" (p. 46). This is a two-stage process (Freire, 1970). In the first stage, the oppressed learns how to read the world, situating his/her personal story in history, uncovering the structures that create oppression. The oppressed "unveil the world of oppression and through praxis commit themselves to its transformation" (Freire, 1970, p. 54). In the second stage, in the new readable world of the oppressed, the nature of oppression is transformed, changed. It "ceases to belong to [just] the oppressed" (p. 54). The pedagogy of oppression has been inverted "through the expulsion of the myths created and developed in the old order, which like specters haunt the new structure emerging from the revolutionary transformation" (p. 54). It now "becomes a pedagogy of all people in the process of permanent liberation" (p. 54).

We are fond of Hill's statement: "Our most basic epistemological assumption that knowledge derives from doing presupposes that 'doing' occurs with others" (1998, p. 143). Hence a performance-centered pedagogy uses performance as a method of investigation, as a way of doing inquiry, and as a method of learning and understanding, a manner of cooperatively engaging bodies (students and teachers), in the classroom setting, in recreating the meanings of experience (pp. 142–3).

Invoking the concept of the ideological body, Pineau (1998) argues that "the fusion of critical pedagogy and performance praxis" (p. 130) exposes how educational, ethnographic, and performing bodies are disciplined and ideologically trained in the classroom and in society at large (p. 128). In this sense, a critical performative pedagogy, to use Pineau's term, works outward from the university and its classrooms treating these spaces as critical public spheres. It creates possibilities for teachers and students alike to see these academic spaces as sites for resistance and empowerment in a performative way, which permits the discourse created there to be transportable to other classrooms and universities, where a revolutionary utopianism is imagined and experienced.

Within this radical pedagogical space, the performative and the political intersect on the concrete relationship of bodies. Denzin (2009) reminds us that the pedagogical is always ideological, always political, and always already performative. And performances, if critical in this sense, can disrupt hegemonic educational practices that subjugate those outside the circle of us (Giroux & Giroux, 2005). In this model, performative critical pedagogy, the traditionally excluded finds the possibility of becoming autoethnographic. The teacher's and student's bodies, especially when coming from positions of oppression, become justified. No, it is not only a personal story, a biography, anymore. Using a critical imagination, the autoethnographer theoretically links biography and history. The narratives created by the oppressed betweener body "must always be directed back to the structures that shape and produce the violence in question" (Denzin, 2003, p. 239).

Few of those bodies, are teaching (Ellis, 2004).

The betweener body, the body that more often than not is missing from the pedagogical space, creates performances that are putting in check the producers of power and knowledge. It becomes an act of doing, being, and knowing, in a concrete moment, constructed in local subjugated knowledges at the bottom of social hierarchies. In pedagogical performative stages, like the classroom, these autoethnographies help create concrete spaces where hopeful performances can be experienced.

We took one of Pineau's (1998) questions to heart: "What emerges if we take schooling the body as the conceptual point of entry into educational research?" (p. 128). We are trying to answer Pineau's call.

Glimpse 8: The Student

I am in my second year in high school. I am attending this nice private school, not the top in my city, but good enough where I can hope to attend college someday. Here (Brasil) it is almost impossible to land in a college coming from the trashed public educational system. Grandma is so happy and proud. We don't have the money to afford such a school but I am going for free! Here is the deal; I play basketball for the club in my city. The school, Anglo, has its name on our jerseys, and so I go to school for free.

I have long days. Wake up at 6:00 am, arrive at school at 7:30 (long walk from home), stay until 12:30, then another long walk, I should say long run, to be at work by 1:00 pm. Work until 6:30 pm, then another run to basketball practice from 7 to 9:30 pm, and then another long walk (are you tired yet?) to get home. It could be worse and, plus, as I said before, Grandma is so happy! Her smile is worth all this. In addition, education should provide a way out, right? Who knows? Depending on my work ethic, I may end up as a professor or cleaning bathrooms.

It's the end of our short recess. I've been hanging out with two friends (my teammates). Not all the players attend school here. In soccer-land, basketball is an elite sport. So it is just four of us who don't pay for the school. However, just Everson and I are flat-out poor.

We got to the classroom a little late, but the teacher is not there. I can sense a buzz in the air. "Someone took money from the cafeteria," I heard someone say. Almost at the same time the secretary is at the door: "Claudio, the principal wants to talk to you. May you please come with me?"

Hey, nothing new here. Every time there is a problem, I get called to the principal's office. The usual suspect. I get into fights, I am not friendly with the other students, don't dress appropriately. For years, I worked in a tractor factory, so my clothes were spotted with oil and grease. I smelled of oil and grease.

I enter the principal's office and stand in front of his desk. He is busy with paperwork.

He puts the papers way and looks at me.

"Claudio... Claudio. Someone took some money from the register at the cafeteria this morning."

I look at him and say nothing.

"I expect that if you knew something you would tell me, right?"

I just nod and remain in silence.

"You are aware that if you know something this is the time to tell me... so it can end here, inside this room."

I remain in silence.

"You have been missing school lately, getting into fights."

"Have got in no fights for months," I say.

"I tried to call your house but..."

"Phone is disconnected. We have not paid the bill... sir."

"I need to contact someone from your house."

"I am splitting time between Grandma and Uncle Paulo's house. The other phone in my file belongs to Uncle Paulo," I say

"Are you sure you don't have anything to say to me?"

"Yes."

"You may leave now."

I start to walk away and then I stop. Looking at the principal, I say:

"Sir, Uncle Paulo is a big, physical man with a very short temper. He adores me and I can't do no wrong in his eyes. He doesn't take shit from no one."

I turn around and walk away as fast I can.

If Uncle Paulo finds out that I've been skipping classes, I am in deep, deep shit. I doubt Mister Motherfucker will contact him unless he knows for sure I took the money.

The phone call never came.

"Hey yo, how about you? Do you also think I took the money?"

Glimpse 9: The Privileged's Question

"Why is Claudio so angry?"

Glimpse 10: "The Flesh"

We just refuse to erase the flesh from the study/understanding of being human. We can only experience the world through a very specific physical location: our bodies (Diversi and Moreira, 2009, p. 31). We sense and perceive the world before we try to make sense of it (Merleau-Ponty, 1969). And we sense and perceive the world with and through our bodies, our flesh, our physical position in the world. Here, again, as betweeners in cultural and ethnic identities, we resonate with Anzaldúa's and Lorde's call for the inclusion of visceral knowledge in the scholarly composition about oppression and discrimination.

We believe that knowledge, specifically knowledge about the Other, is always produced by a situated body as it, the body, interacts with other bodies and the surrounding environment, such as the classroom and school's hallways. It's a way to point out where the teaching/ethnography's navel is and the kind of bodies that, more often than not, teach, and the kind that get schooled.

Glimpse 11: The Betweener Body in the Academic Space

When I came to my interview at the University of Massachusetts (U Mass) I could feel the tension in the department. It became very clear to me that there was a group of faculty that did not want a hire in performance studies. There was tension in the air. To be clear, they weren't against me, personally. They did not want the hire to happen, regardless of the candidate.

Professors walked away in the middle of my job talk.

Once I got hired, and I entered that space, I became the tension. One thing is to criticize one of my texts. Another is to have the betweener body, me, teaching, my flesh, viscera, blood, in "their" classroom. The threatening body… who does not fit… who loves and cares… who shits and pisses… walking in the hallway… being harassed by the Po-lice and full professors… disrupting the academic space… I feel, I am the incarnation of a scholarship trying to break free from colonialism. My body, not simply what I do, challenges the basic assumptions of the "right" kind of scholarship.

My mother tells me:

"It's so ironic… you never, ever liked school and here you are, a teacher!"

"Mom," I answer with a big grin, "I am indeed a teacher but I still don't like school."

Claudio, you have to write a theoretical paper.

What have I been writing, then?

The joy, when Emily Polk, a brilliant human being, says in my grad seminar, after eight weeks, where I intentionally downplay the role of theory:

Polky: "Wait a minute! This autoethnographic writing is extremely theoretical."

Assumptions…

Glimpse 12: Decolonizing Pedagogies

I enter the classroom. Students are already waiting for me, sitting in a circle. I time myself to be a few minutes late. I carry a chair to the middle of the room.

The public pedagogical space of the classroom…

I don't say a word.

I place my water bottle and coffee on the chair. Do the same with my new leather black trench coat, my knitted cap, and sunglasses... I handle a student the Holman Jones article "Autoethnography: Making the Personal Political" we were to have read for class today. Passages are circled and numbered.

"Good morning beautiful people [my usual greeting; it is 1 o'clock in the afternoon]."

Students are looking at me... I say:

"Stacey Holman Jones asks to not read her text alone... I am asking you to stand up. I am inviting all of us to perform a story... for us. Whenever I pause to drink water or take a sip of my coffee you are to read a passage from the text and then pass it to another person to do the same at the next pause. Each time, after one of you finishes reading, you will all move a step forward.

Ready?"

Last year when I got to U Mass one conversation with a colleague stayed with me. This friend tells me that she had another professor, a Black woman, invited to her class to talk about race... At a certain point, that professor was challenged by a student: "You cannot be oppressed on campus anymore; you're a professor." The professor, the invited woman of color, answers: "Yes, here in the classroom, I am the professor, but later today, when it is dark, at the bus stop, I am only another Black woman."

I stop to drink water.

The next moment of qualitative inquiry will be one at which the practices of qualitative research finally move, without hesitation or encumbrance, from the personal to the political (Denzin, 2000, p. 261; quoted from Holman Jones, 2005, p. 763).

"Many years ago, when I first got to this country, without any English, I was a janitor at 'the great' University of Illinois. My fore*man* was a woman. How can I learn English? I ask When, the foreman is a woman?" Students laugh.

"Anyway, my boss tells me to sweep the outside stairs of the fancy Alumni Building."

"Claudio, it is an important building; it's where the university brings its donors... It is locked after hours, lots of money in there, so you go to the Union if you need water or a bathroom break."

"Here I am, using my broom, sweeping the stairs of this fancy building. I hear voices yelling at me. I turn around and there are three yelling cops with their guns pointing at me."

This chapter is about the personal text as critical intervention in social, political, and cultural life. Please, do not read it alone (Holman Jones, 2005, p. 763).

"So... so scared. Can't understand a word of what they are saying... my English is so broken. I heard the sound of the broom. I have the broom close to my chest in a kind of defensive position... what's going on here?

Shaking, sweating, scared... shitless scared!

With tears on my face I throw the broom on the floor and starting saying: Janitor, janitor, janitor...

In my thoughts:

I am only the janitor... I am just cleaning this fancy building of yours.

Later, I don't know how much later, my boss, the forewoman, tells me that someone from inside the building called about this suspicious individual on the stairs... pretending to sweep...

'Haven't those stairs been swept before?'

Am I so different from the other janitors?"

Pause for coffee

> This chapter is more than a little utopian in its call to disrupt, produce, and imagine a breakthrough in – and not a respite from – the way things are and perhaps should be (Ricoeur, 1986, pp. 265–6). It cannot stand alone in the world (Holman Jones, 2005, p. 763).

"Beautiful people, I was just cleaning... was that the first time that a janitor was sweeping those stairs? Was my broom a weapon of mass destruction? Hey, we never know... we went to war for less than that...

Anyway, two days ago, Wednesday, there was a faculty meeting on Campus Center (CC), have you been to CC?"

Some nods, expressing "of course, yes", some laugh... what's the point?

"Do you know that there is a bathroom in the basement of CC? After you pass the bank?"

More nods...

"Okay, after a faculty meeting, I really needed to go the bathroom."

At this moment I move myself from the center to the circle pretending to be a student.

"Hey Claudio," I say, "I understand you write this autoethnography and stuff, but really we don't need to know when you want to go potty."

Laughs, and I move back to the center of the circle.

"Really, don't you need to know? I bet in this case you do... embodiment of our sociological imagination... let's bring biography and history into play."

"I have kids, folks, every time I go to the bathroom at home one of them is knocking on the door. I just want it quiet, know what I mean?" More laughs. "Have it all planned, I am going to go potty, as my kids say, in the basement of the CC. No biggy, right?"

> This is a chapter about how looking at the world from a specific, perspectival, and limited vantage point can tell, teach, and put people in motion (Holman Jones, 2005, p. 763).

68 Betweenness in Systemic Exclusion

"I get away from the escalator. I notice some kind of commotion far away on my right side but don't pay much attention. I turn left; pass a man wearing a suit and tie, right in front of the bank. I nod to him and get no answer. I enter the bathroom. I want quiet so I go to the last toilet on the far right.

After 5, 10 minutes... don't know for sure... there is a strong bang on the toilet door.

BAM, BAM, BAM, BAM...

The voice comes like a thunder:

'Get out of there! You're taking too long!'

'What?' I babble.

Not knowing, not knowing!

The thunder again

'Get out of there! You're taking too long! Police Department!'"

I look at the students' faces around me. I can see the shock stamped on them. I sip my coffee

> *It is about autoethnography as a radical democratic politics – a politics committed to creating space for dialogue and debate that instigates and shapes social change (Reinelt, 1998, p. 286). It does not act alone (Holman Jones, 2005, p. 763).*

"I can barely pull up my pants. I am shaking...

'Get out of there!'

The thunder again.

I open the door. Two detectives in civilian clothes are looking at me, holding up their badges.

'Who are you? You don't look like a student. You're too old.'

Thoughts, memories, come flying through my body

Relief that my family is not witnessing this

I wanna tell you how tough and Brazilian macho I am

But no

I am scared

Shaking

Sweating

It literally smells bad in here

Right now, performing at this moment, my jaw is locked with rage

I am in pain

Embarrassed

In fear

'I... I am a p... professor here,' I stutter."

> *This is a chapter about how a personal text can move writers and readers, subjects and objects, teller and listeners into a space of a dialogue, debate, and change. It does not speak alone. (Holman Jones, 2005, p. 764).*

"'I... am a p... professor here.'

At this moment... the face... the cop's face showing that look, so familiar in my history

That look... that face... you know... kind of

'Nice try, but who are you?' That look, you know?"

Turning around, and looking each student in the eye, I interrupt the story and say:

"Please, remember beautiful people, we are not looking for Truth here. We are performing the past not to 'recognize it the way it really was,' but 'to seize hold of a memory as it flashes up at a moment of danger' (Benjamin, 1968, p. 257), to embody and recreate the past not as a succession of events, but as a series of scenes, inventions, emotions, images, and stories (Ulmer, 1989). We seek a performance, true or not quite true, that must be just and right... that must create a space with more dignity and respect for more people... not only to the ones who look like us... that must create a pedagogy of hope, care, and love (Darder, 2002, p. 32). We are, right now, historicizing the body quoting history back to itself. In bringing memories into the public, political, pedagogical, and physical space of the classroom, I insert myself into the past and invite you, together, 'to create the conditions for rewriting and hence re-experiencing it' (Denzin, 2009, p. 334)."

Stopping and moving back to center, I continue.

"'Please, step over there,' strongly says one of the detectives pointing in the direction of the mirrors.

'Do you have identification on you?' he asks.

'Yes.'

'May I have it?'

'May I wash my hands first... sir?' I ask."

> *Setting a scene, telling a story, carefully constructing the connections between life and art, experience and theory, evocation and explanation... and then letting go, hoping for readers who will bring the same careful attention to your words in the context of their own lives (Holman Jones, 2005, p. 765).*

"Washing my hands, my heart seems to be ready to implode inside my chest. I am drenched in sweat. My hands don't stop shaking. Trembling, I give the detective my driver's license and university ID.

'Let's step outside the bathroom,' says the one I gave my ID to.

Outside the bathroom, in an open view, embarrassment again occurs, is renewed

Fear is reinforced

Again the relief that my family is not present

The detective walks away with my IDs and stops to talk with the man in a suit and tie, which I nodded to when I first got in the bathroom. The other cop stays with me and starts a new line of questioning.

'So, you are a professor here?'
'Yes.'
'In which department?'
'Communication.'
'In which building?'
'Machmer Hall.'

I am still shaking. My voice is still trembling. Carefully, I look past the detective talking to me and see the other cop on his radio, while the man in a suit and tie with his moving mouth is saying something to him.

A lifetime of getting in trouble with the Po-lice is passing through my mind.

What is happening now? Holman Jones asks us to not read it alone, I ask you to stand up and, step by step, to get closer to each other... I am not asking for a book understanding... I am inviting you for a bodily interaction, a human allegiance, of sharing emotions and re-experiencing contested meanings."

> Making a text present. Demanding attention and participation. Implicating all involved. Refusing closure or categorization (Holman Jones, 2005, p. 765).

"There was a complaint about three individuals harassing students down here in the basement. We already apprehended two of them. The description of the third one was a person with a long leather black trench coat, with a black hat, and facial hair." While I am saying these words I put on my coat and hat.

"I do not give the detective an answer right away. I wait a little and say:
'So, a long leather black trench coat... very suspicious right?'

The detective looks me in the eye, makes an expression that seems to mean no.

'There is a misunderstanding here. Wait a minute, please, SIR.' And he walks away to talk with the other detective and the person in the suit and tie.

'See,' I say, 'I become Sir.'

Now, the three of them are talking. I try to read their lips and body expressions. I try to keep my body straight. Time? I don't know... a minute or two... my whole life... in any case, it is a minute or two too long!

Why, beautiful people, why?" I say, turning my body around in the middle of the small circle, looking at all of my students. I can feel that at this moment the students and I are holding each others' backs. There is synchrony, one of these moments in the classroom that clicks. I see teary eyes... I have teary eyes... we're together in this moment.

"Not why the cops, the Po-lice came after me; not why they could not wait until I finish...

Shit

But why did I invite you to this performance? Why are we performing in the classroom?"

> *Witnessing experience and testifying about power without foreclosure – of pleasure, of difference, of efficacy (Holman Jones, 2005, p. 765).*

"They are coming back towards me. One of the detectives says,
'We are very sorry, sir. We have the description and it matches you.'
'Yes,' adds the other, 'we're sorry. Just doing our job.'
The man in the suit and tie gets closer. Now I can tell that he is some kind of administrator in the campus center, a U Mass employee.
'I am sorry sir. But the description was of an individual in a long leather black trench coat, with a black hat, and facial hair. It is… just like you.'
'Do I take it as compliment, sir?' I ask.
'Okay, next time you come here, I'll give you a cup of coffee?'
'What? Next time I come here? I work here! Don't you have that squared out?'
Still shaking, I ask looking now at the cops. 'A cup of coffee, no sir, thank you. I have a coffee maker in my office… May I go now?' I ask the detectives.
'Of course, sir. Again we are sorry. Have a good day.'
'Good day…' I say and walk away.
Beautiful people. Here now, in this classroom. I have some kind of control. My body has some kind of legitimacy. But how about when I go to the bathroom? How about when the African American professor, a woman, is at the bus stop in the dark?
As the detective reminds us, after banging on the toilet door, I do not look like a professor.
Or a student, for that matter!
'Beautiful people,' I say, turning around and looking at all the students, 'am I asking too much of our educational system to be able to teach, do research, and use the bathroom in the place I labor without having to be harassed for my looks?'
'Shit,' I yell and start to drink water.

> *Believing that words matter and writing toward the moment when the point of creating autoethnographic texts is to change the world (Holman Jones, 2005, p. 765).*

I look at my watch and it is time to end the performance. I want to give some time for the students to decompress and, if possible, to bring a smile back to their faces. Also, I want them to have time to talk to me if they wish to. I am responsible for the emotions flying in this classroom.
"Beautiful people, I am not asking for your pity. I am not telling you this so you may feel sorry for me. Remember, after 40 minutes or so, they were apologizing to me. I am a professor after all," I say, with a smile on my face.
"But I am still the janitor, too.
Whose bodies are safe at this university, and under what circumstances?

Whose bodies are missing?

We are ending here. Thank you for participating. Next class, we will talk about what we have just done."

The students begin to pack.

"Just remember: The bathroom at the basement of CC may not be a safe place," I say.

Amid some laughter, they start to leave the classroom.

Glimpse 13: The Master's Tools Can't Remedy the Exclusion of Missing Bodies in Academia

We are claiming here that the Master's Tools – the privileging of theoretical and linguistically sophisticated analysis of oppression over visceral experiences of oppression expressed in colloquial language and from a biographical standpoint – cannot help us address the integrated-but-not-equal injustice of American education. By insisting on representing the Other from an omnipotent perspective (i.e., the unilateral expert theorizing of Others' experiences), educators of all walks of life continue to subjugate, however unwittingly, students into dehumanizing categories of self. And we believe this approach affects everyone in exclusionary ways. For those students who see themselves in the mainstream categories, the experience of oppression is less visceral and, thus, less connected with the status quo. As a result, the state of inequality in society at large and education in particular is largely due to individuals' shortcomings, with little to no consideration of social structure and circumstance. And the consequences of this sociological imagination are more direct than the superficial impression. Those with a history of privileged representations and experiences (i.e., less dehumanizing) will likely have greater power over their counterparts via affluence and narrative space. Few teachers, professors, lawyers, physicians, journalists, and politicians have come from the visceral worlds of oppression. Yet they continue to insist on their own single story on how to promote equality in any number of social arenas.

Ah, education! For those students who, early on and with a daily barrage, experience social exclusion and dehumanizing representations, education is often an obvious Master's Tool to justify inequality as a result of personal weakness and limitation. In this light, we believe that alienation from education is not an act of disinterest but an act of active resistance.

We are proposing, here and in our classrooms and scholarly writings, that one way of expanding the circle of inclusion in education is by insisting on a pedagogy and representation of the Other that honor visceral, bodily situated experiences of exclusion beyond the colonized role of samples and informants.

We are hoping that decolonizing pedagogies and scholarship can help us not only dismantle the Master's House of exclusion, but also co-construct with the Other a house more inclusive of more people by way of visceral resonance.

Glimpse 14: The Afterwards Professor

I have revisited the experience. I get angry, ashamed... I feel embarrassed and can't let it go... I try to justify the police actions... powerless and humiliated... until when? I keep asking no one. Something broke at that moment... there was joy of coming to work every morning at U Mass... of being a professor... it has been gone since... the blessing of the dream... or it may be the curse.

A few days later I go to the bathroom at the recreation center... I do not want quiet... I do not want to be alone in a *public bathroom* at U Mass... I sit down on the toilet... something is wrong... don't know exactly what... when I bring my hands to my face, kind of a desperation move, they, my hands, get wet.

Migrant Stories

I am
We are the
Borders we cross
The places we live and labor

How Far from Where We Fall in?

As migrating human beings, we find our very existence, simple as it is in the larger scheme of things, constantly being represented as the Other, the different, the outsider, the foreigner, the accented, not part of Us, part of Them, and seldom in a kind way. Right, wrong, in-between, or both, we believe this is a common experience of a large part of the billions in humankind. And who isn't directly related to someone from someplace else?

How far from the spot on which we plop upon arrival till we qualify as a migrant on this planet?

Ten feet to the washing basin?

Ten miles to school?

Tens of borders away from your first place on earth?

How far from where we first touch the earth till we can justify the exclusion of fellow human beings on the fleeting base of belonging to a land?

That assumes, beyond all reason
And kindness,
That any chunk of land can belong to any of us
Till "us" means everyone.

Learning English

The year is 1999. I am in my reading English class. The teacher is introducing new words in our limited vocabulary in English. It is a basic exercise. The teacher reads the word aloud and we, the students, try to guess the meaning.

"Alien," the teacher says
I raise my hand very fast. I know the word.
"Claudio, go ahead."
"Monster! Alien is a monster!" I say with confidence.
Dan, the teacher has a funny smile on his face.
"A monster? Are you sure, Claudio?"
"Yes, I watched the movie… with Sigourney… can't pronounce her name…"
Dan is still wearing his smile.
"Yes Claudio, it may be a monster like in the movie, but it is also you."
"Me? I am not that thing! I am a human being."

Local Immigrants

I've recently moved to a new community. Once again, I've encountered the familiar things of life in a new place: not knowing where to go for food, not knowing anyone to ask. New streets, new blind spots, new local corks. This newness has always been more pleasure than pain for me. Even getting lost in a new city is appealing to me, like an adventure with few serious threats beyond other human beings. Needless to say, I have been lucky to move to places I've chosen, always with privileged resources and back-up plans.

But I've always felt a bit bad about arriving with suitcases. New cities are already too crowded. People all around seem to know where they are going. Young, old, and otherwise appear to carry on with a sense of familiarity I don't have. I can't suppress the feeling that I am butting in, invading their land, one more body in line, interrupting their daily bustle with questions about the obvious. Excuse me sir, ma'am, where is the post office? A simple question like that is often enough for the immediate establishment of a dualistic relationship of Us and Them, insider and outsider, local and migrant. The tension rests on how the local responds to the sudden recognition of a migrant.

This time, I was moving to an allegedly progressive place, the Pacific Northwest. I wasn't sure what my friends meant by "progressive," but I must have imagined, uncritically, some notion about this being a more inclusive community. At the more conscious level, I knew Pacific Northwesterners were, well, people. But somewhere between consciousness and daydreaming I thought that everyone I saw walking around in my new community brewed their own beer, ate veggies from their own organic communal garden, raised urban chickens for hormone- and cruelty-free eggs, drove hybrids with Free Tibet bumper stickers, but only when their bicycles were getting tuned up at the co-op around the corner. I bought my first COEXIST t-shirt at the local farmer's market and hoped it made for a good cover.

Then I went to my new faculty orientation. I felt strangely at home as soon as I heard the first statement, a heartfelt welcome to the "Coug family," and a joke about how the joy of being a Coug was heightened by the disastrous year the

Huskies had had. Hearty laughter all around. The room felt warmer. Alliances were clear. I hadn't known who the Huskies were until that very moment. But the "them" was framed so incisively that I immediately knew it had to be my university's main competitor in the legislature, the mightier University of Washington.

In no time I started hearing other local us-versus-themisms that grabbed my migrant attention: Washington residents have repeatedly voted against a light rail line across the Columbia River, a mass transportation option that would greatly improve the quality of living of tens of thousands of Washington residents who fight the brutal bottleneck of the two bridges into Portland, where they work. According to the *Columbian*, the local newspaper, the number one reason for the "no" vote has been the same each time: Washington residents don't want "them," Portlanders, bringing their tattoos, piercings, colored hairdos, queerness, and, God forbid, their tree-hugging tendencies over to "our" side, the good side.

Like in the rest of the country, immigration is a vivid site of us-versus-them discourse in my new community. Latinos are competing with "our" kids for the already scarce school resources. Russians are doing the same, but by *not* sending "their" kids to school. Fellow Americans moving from other states bring "their" liberal ideas and drive prices out of range for "our" families.

Much of this resentment is shared openly and in the self-righteous tones of those who have long forgotten their own migrant journey here. Lewis and Clark are celebrated for opening a migration path to the region for "their" ancestors, the migrant ancestors of the local people.

The centerpiece of the downtown park in my new community is a stylized totem pole honoring the indigenous people who first welcomed Lewis and Clark in 1804. I stood facing the totem pole that first day at the park, listening to the recorded sage-sounding voice coming out of it, accompanied by faint drum beats, a voice that described the importance of the salmon swimming up and down the Columbia River for the many tribes that lived at its margins for thousands of years. Not too far away from the totem pole is a bronze statue of the European soldier who founded the town in 1825. His name was George Vancouver. I could see George from the same spot I stood listening to the totem pole speak and rolled my eyes.

And HOW could I NOT roll my eyes before such sad irony? It's like a Thanksgiving déjà vu, West Coast version. Now that they are no longer part of the troubling "them," the native can be celebrated as part of "us," part of "our" heritage, the generous people who shared turkey and salmon with "us" when "we" needed the most.

I roll my eyes and shake my head. How can "they" be so hypocritical and not even see it?!

And then, I hear it. "They?" I hear my own voice echoing inside my head.

Ah, the chill of catching oneself in that act. The chill of catching MYself being indignant about "their" hypocritical display of us-versus-themism!

I recover my balance between acceptance of what I believe is an inseparable part of my human condition, that is, seeing the world in simpler categories whenever possible, and a renewed desire to further explore ways in which we can develop educational systems that bring a Freirean level of conscientização to mind more easily. If we can't get rid of dualistic tendencies, as I believe, may we at least find ways to be better at identifying it in ourselves, in our so-called decolonizing acts. *Before* we try to decolonize others.

Monsters, kind of

I am not that monster am I?
I am a human being am I not?
I am
We are the
Borders we cross
The place we live and labor
I want to teach English in Arizona
I am the hybrid monster/human
The Alien in Sigourney Weaver/Warrant Officer Ripley's womb
Do I look illegal to you?

★★★

the real question about the utility of the old Platonic dualisms is whether or not their deployment weakens our sense of human solidarity. I read Dewey as saying that discarding these dualisms will help bring us together, by enabling us to realize that trust, social cooperation and social hope are where our humanity begins and ends.

(Rorty, 1999, p. xv)

Fellow Brazilians

I am going to vote. In the Left of course. I vote for Dilma!
You should not vote, especially for her! You don't live here! You have no right!
Outsider!
Traitor!
If you care that much why you don't fucking live here?
Many answers...
I don't know!

Bodies and Borders, Body as Border

Moving bodies diasporic
Invading the Brazilian Dream of a melting pot of foreign stock harmony in
  America!

Well-Intentioned Essentializing Assumptions of Immigrants

"You should be very proud of yourself," a friendly student recently told me as we walked through the quad after class.

"What do you mean?" I ask a bit surprised.

"Well, look at you, you came a long way from the tough hand you were dealt. And now you are a college professor in America," he says with a light squeeze of my arm.

"Tough hand I was dealt?" I ask.

"Yeah, growing up in, er... the Third World and all," he says.

"It's nice of you to offer this compliment. But I can't accept it in good conscience."

"I don't mean any disrespect, I promise," he says interrupting me and suddenly looking a bit nervous.

"No offense taken, please, don't worry," I add quickly, "it's just that I had a very privileged upbringing in Brazil, attending high-quality private schools all the way up to college, living with great comfort, supported by a thoughtful and supportive family, lacking for nothing. I got handed an easy hand, truly. Don't you remember me talking about all this on the first day of class? I remember you being there."

"Uh, now that you mention it, I do... but I guess my image of the Third World trumped what you said that day... sorry," he says, looking a bit dejected. Or embarrassed. I can't really tell.

"Active listening can be hard," I say, trying to make a hook with a concept we discussed in a recent class on communicative strategies, trying to let him off the other hook.

We part with a good handshake and smiles. I am glad we got a chance to have this exchange. I should make a greater effort to position my Brazilian upbringing in relation to my students' assumptions about Brazil in particular, and the Third World in general. I should also share some of my own misassumptions of Others as an attempt to create narratives of commonality in our struggles to overcome binary linguistic traps of us-themisms.

Isn't that the only way we come to empathize with Others?

By finally being able to see ourselves in the Other's shoes?

Perhaps, I wonder as I walk back to my office, Steve will pause to ponder alternative possibilities of identity next time he meets someone from the Third World. And I sure hope I will carry the memories of this encounter next time I have uncritical impulses to essentialize my own Others.

Possibilities...

The Hybrid Monster/Human

I

    The Alien in Sigourney Weaver/Warrant Officer Ripley's womb
    May be not

It may be my English teacher is right after all… were I to be that monster, people in the only America would understand me/us fellow migrants.

Were I that monster, violent, cruel, and powerful, America would get us… respect us. The language of violence is clearly understood by the big bully in the world. Violence is the universal language of the empire.

However,
We still are that kind of monster or maybe
Another kind
Hybrid monster/human product of colonial rape
Betweeners
Not violent for sure unless when we use our embodied words
The words are accusatory for sure but only of the system that insists on carnal narratives, strong accent, lack of intelligence, and work ethic
Lack of loyalty to country and family and gratitude to the American way of life all mixed in a humungous state of dumbness
Surprise: we're not that dumb
Some of us are poor
Some of us can pass – keep your mouth shut
Some of us Brown, Black, kinda White, Pardo,
Or borrowing from Gloria Anzaldúa in her vision of "El Mundo Zurdo" – The Left Hand World.
"Some of us are leftists, some of us practitioners of magic. Some of us are both" (Moraga & Anzaldúa, 1981, p. 209).
Some of us are
Our people
Your maids, drivers, caretakers, workers, killers, thieves, robbers, refugees
And even if for a few times,
Your teachers… not being productive and drinking the government milk
Being… such lazy asses
We are not scary, are we?
Were we ripping off people from their own
STOMACH
Not in the belly of the beast but
The Beast in the belly
Killing whatever is in front of us along the way we would at least be
Understood if not respected, even if it comes by fear
Isn't that what America does to the
Other?
Killing and chaos in other places
Vietnam and other places in Asia, the Middle East, South and Central America, Western Europe.

★★★

The title "Hope in Place of Knowledge" is a way of suggesting that Plato and Aristotle were wrong in thinking that humankind's most distinctive and praiseworthy capacity is to know things as they really are – to penetrate behind appearance to reality. That claim saddles us with the unfortunate appearance–reality distinction and with metaphysics: a distinction, and a discipline, which pragmatism shows us how to do without. I want to demote the quest for knowledge from the status of end-in-itself to that of one more means toward greater human happiness.

(Rorty, 1999, p. xiii)

Why We Left

Why did we leave our "home" country?
  Growing up poor in Brazil is not a good
  Thing
I've been in the USA for almost 12 years, all of them as a visa holder. Especially after the "Patriotic Act," as a visa carrier, I have no rights whatsoever, and yet... Citizenship is a concept I experience in the USA. I could not vote for Obama as I did for Dilma and yet
  My whole life in Brasil was marked by disdain, a third-class kinda person not ever, not
  Ever
  Not once a citizen.
  I was 10 or 11 and worked illegally in Brasil. I got paid half of the minimum wage!
  Always
  Half of the minimum
  Half of self
  Half of person
  Half of being
  Yet a whole monster
  That kinda monster with
  With feelings of... gratitude!
  As Grandma usually reminded me:
  "You got a job; thousands don't."
  Gratitude? Just kiss my beautiful behind!
  Why I left?
  We're the monsters there... not much difference after all. Don't trust me? Go ahead and ask any illegal Bolivian living in São Paulo City. Try this and then tell how their stories differ from the illegal here in this country.
  São Paulo and New York, the same side of a different coin!

Toward Narratives of Healing and Social Hope

We experience life in-between cultures, ethnicities, class, and indigenousness. In Brazil, where we grew up and now go back to for family and research, we are white. In the USA, where we live and labor, we are brown, at least off-white. In Brazil, we are often treated as migrants who have chosen to leave their country of origin and are, at best, outsiders. In the heat of an argument with friends and family about politics, we are called traitors for having left the motherland. In the USA, we are often treated as migrants with a deficit in language, intelligence, and loyalty to country and family. Sometimes we are treated worse, of course. But who isn't? And who doesn't treat others worse than we could? We know we don't have a privileged vantage point on this.

But we speak from a common vantage point, the migrant vantage point. We speak as migrants who weren't migrants until the beginning of our adult lives. We speak as migrants who didn't think much about migrants until we felt the insufferable arrogance and hypocrisy of locals. We speak as migrants who are trying to face our own migrantphobias in the mirror.

"You are welcome to my country!" we have heard from locals who appear to be trying to express warmth and friendship. But these parochial greeters can't see the appalling divisiveness in the gesture. The relationship is immediately gelled into an Us/Them opposition, where the differences are elevated as the relational parameters. And important commonalities vanish in the background. The benign local who shares words of welcome, words that in their very utterance claim higher rights of belonging at the expense of another's basic human right to feel at home anywhere on the planet, positions himself (we have only had men say this to us) as the unalienable owner of the land where we now stand. It's a backdoor reminder that migrants don't enjoy the same rights as locals. To ask such locals whether they, also, were greeted by the previous locals upon their migrant arrival would be too impolite for our taste. So we turn our gaze and critique toward larger structures and narratives that make it possible for this historical forgetfulness to be so ingrained in the sociological imagination in the first place.

While we can do wondrous things in the 21st century, we are still largely deprived of narratives of possibility for human connection. We are starved of narratives of inclusion so powerful that over time they become more appealing than narratives of exclusion. New Americans instead of legal aliens or foreign stock, say.

We realize this experience of life in-between, where exclusion is too frequent for comfort, isn't unique to us. And we believe that autoethnographies of immigration can be used as a site of possibility for narratives of life in-between local and foreign. We offer these thoughts as a way of resisting the persistent colonizing discourse about the Other. As a way of seeking healing through emotional connection with the Other through narratives that resonate with each of our own migrant experiences of the world. We believe autoethnographies of immigration can offer readers glimpses into Others' lives that bridge common human experiences of wanting to improve our lot, to belong to larger groups and larger causes, to live meaningful lives. Glimpses that create visceral connection with Others because you could see yourself in the Others' shoes, if only for a brief instant. We attempt to write narratives where the circle of Us becomes more inclusive and the circle of Them becomes harder to justify.

We share autoethnographies of our encounters with the many forces and identities of immigration, both inclusive and exclusionary, with the explicit intent to resist and trouble the persistent single story of the outsider. This single story has been told, particularly in formal education, from the arrogant pedestal of self-proclaimed expertise. It's a view from everywhere, or from objectivity, as the single story experts claim. In our view as accidental immigrants, this theoretical expertise of the Other, of the immigrant, is toxic and exclusionary, regardless of the expert's ethical protestations to the contrary. In the spirit of resistance against ideologies of domination via theoretical expertise and of healing through shared narratives of life as betweeners, we stand on the shoulders of inclusionary performers to try and create representational mirrors of our own encounter with diaspora – situated, subjective, and partial.

Just as encounters with the Other always are.
We are not erasing the history of forced migration
Slavery, refugees, to name a few
Nor are we sugarcoating the bloodbath of colonial rape
In bodies of color
Nor trying to clean the sanguine fluid in the hands of the white European man
Nor turning a blind eye to the imperialistic project of corporations
The new colonial force of our times
Disguised as corporations promoting "free" trade
While pushing indigenous peoples out of their homelands
Invariably run by modern conquistadores
Diaspora always includes some kind of loss
Home, land, identity…
Instead we gain Dark Red memories
Blood
Bodies
But We are dangerous to power! (Madison, 2009). And
Like Gloria Anzaldúa (1987/1999), we ask to be met halfway
There, we may have a dialogue
In the halfway place
We must find
Ways
To realize we

Are
Migrant locals
On this planet
Rise up!

Note

1 We have worked with Brazilian street youth, sugar cane workers, organized soccer fan clubs, and undocumented immigrants in the U.S.A. in our own individual research projects (see Diversi & Moreira, 2009 for more details).

5
BETWEENNESS IN DECOLONIZING INQUIRY

Classrooms as Decolonizing Sites

The cynicism that embraces the notion that changes are impossible or too costly (Freire, 1995/2004) is a constant in our battlegrounds: academia, classrooms, scholarship, and praxis of everyday life. "What can we (intellectuals) do to help people in the real world?" is a question we face quite often from colleagues and students alike. We often pause for a moment before this question, not only because the answer requires time and sustained engagement from the part of the questioner, but mostly because our reaction to the basic assumptions that there is a "real world" out there and that the classroom is not part of it require deeper dialogue, as all ideas of ever inclusive social change do. "Wait a minute here, are you saying that 'this' classroom is not real? Or, are you implying that a classroom is somehow separated from the world we inhabit?" As betweener (hybrid, mutt, in-between, either/or) instructors inside the always personal, political, pedagogical, and performative space of the classroom, we reject the old yet pervasive binary narratives of reality from old and new colonizing constructions. And neoliberalism, especially in its public mask, controls the new colonizing constructions of the world order.

Alongside Richard Rorty (1999), Paulo Freire (1970), Gloria Anzaldúa (1999), Frantz Fanon (1952/2007), Norman Denzin (2010), and many others who have openly criticized either/or narratives at the service of oppression against the Other, we refute the notion that the classroom is not part of the "real world." Any educational setting is part of the real world. The same power relations shaping and informing the real world are present in the classroom. The same neoliberal narratives shaping the "new" real world are present in the classroom: Profit over people (Chomsky, 1999), west over east (Said, 1978), north over south, men over women, straight over LGBTQA, White over everyone else, science over arts and humanities, material and energy consumption over ecosystems. And as part of the real world, the classroom and intellectualism need to continue to be sites of resistance and hope against the neoliberal world order of the early 21st century. Like bell hooks taught us in *Teaching to Transgress: Education as the Practice of Freedom* (1994b), we try to make daily connections between the classroom and the history of oppression and resistance.

> Significantly, those of us who are trying to critique biases in the classroom have been compelled to return to the body to speak about ourselves as subjects in history. We are all subjects in history... We must return ourselves to a state of embodiment in order to deconstruct the way power has been traditionally orchestrated in the classroom, denying subjectivity to some groups and according it to others. By recognizing subjectivity and the limits of identity, we disrupt that objectification that is so necessary in a culture of domination.
>
> *(hooks, 1994, p. 139)*

But do allow us to pause a bit and contemplate the narrative strategies so often used to further divide relational sentiments among the masses in the United States. With us or against us. US. versus Them. Intentional polarization frames the portrayal of current events. The wars against Afghanistan, Iraq, and terrorism around the globe can only stand on the shoulders of fear-mongering and a blind sense of patriotic superiority (Chomsky, 2005). "Collateral damage," as an expression, explanation, and excuse, makes invisible the children and innocent bystanders blown to pieces by citizens who insist this is all done in the name of liberty and democracy. Neoliberals talk of liberty and the people accept assault weapons, nothing but killing machines, as *protection* against the government, the Other, the not-good, the not-Us.

Young white men go on mass killing sprees in Oklahoma City, Columbine, Aurora, Newtown and the neoliberal narratives turn the focus to the Other plagued by mental illness dissociated from the world they grew up in, as if mental illness in the United States were not fundamentally connected to a healthcare system more concerned with profit than with people. Look at the Jerry Sandusky sexual abuse scandal in the storied Penn State football program and you can see the signature narrative spins of neoliberalism, itself more concerned with the economic and mythical damage to the Penn State brand than with the many young lives violently interrupted by one of their football heroes (Giardina & Denzin, 2012). The neoliberal control of political and international "news" has become so overwhelming that one only hears about drone strikes in foreign sovereign lands when a drone crashes into "enemy" territory and hands. The multi-year American policy of drone "signature strikes," the pre-emptive bombing of suspicious-looking individuals in Pakistan or Yemen, without reasonable evidence of involvement in terrorism, goes mostly unmentioned, let alone troubled. And when dissenters show evidence of innocent killings, the neoliberal narrative is quick to demonize such dissenters as unpatriotic, traitors to liberty and democracy, truth and honesty be damned.

Neoliberals talk of liberty, and the masses, easily convinced by the narrative of fear and Islamic jihads, keep feeling all right about depriving Guantanamo prisoners of basic rights to a fair trial. President Obama, who the neoliberals attack as leftist/socialist, swore to close Guantanamo during his first campaign in 2008, calling it an affront to American democracy and historical dignity. In May of 2013, already into Obama's second term as president, Gitmo is still open and holding, according to Republican Senator Saxby Chambliss of Georgia at a recent press conference, in response to President Obama's speech in reaction to the widespread detainee hunger strike, "166 of the meanest, nastiest killers in the world" (C-Span, May 23, 2013). By all accounts to date, the vast majority of Gitmo detainees have not been linked to terrorism or any other form of violence or conspiracy against the United States. Even Senator Saxby Chambliss mentions that 86 of the "166 killers" have been cleared for transfer out of Gitmo in the same press release. Yet there, on a corner stolen from the Cuban island many decades ago, so many innocent people linger between limbo and hell based on the neoliberal narrative of "with us or against us," narratives of Arabs as the post-9/11 dark, dangerous, irrationally West-hating Other. Neoliberal narratives of justification talk of liberty that appears to *require* the non-liberty of the Other, domestically and globally.

Anyone with humanist inclinations will want to live in a society where fellow citizens can see through the neoliberal agenda that insists on justifying the sacrifice of the majority for the benefit of the few, through whatever narrative spin its guardians and worshipers try to lay out. We want to live among citizens who will see the neoliberal attempts at diverting the public discourse from systemic inequality to the merits of trickle-down economics and call it bullshit. We want to be inspired by neighbors and strangers who are more concerned with inclusive politics than with talking points that focus all of their might on dehumanizing the Other. Let us live in a world where when one listens to the other side of drone "signature strikes," s/he is forced to re-evaluate preconceived neoliberal assumptions that the United States military is a force for the good. Granted, essential steps have been taken against systems of exclusion of the Other throughout American history. Emancipation declaration, suffrage, American Indian movement, civil rights, feminism of all shades, Occupy Wall Street, A People's History of the United States (Zinn, 1980/2005) – your journeys are not over, but you keep the *sense of us* in search of a "more perfect union" afloat and hopeful.

To us, the classroom has everything to do with examining how the divisive narratives of neoliberalism circulate, get perpetuated, and, hopefully, get challenged. As Paulo Freire pointedly reminds us, "To affirm that men and women are persons and as persons should be free, and yet to do nothing tangible to make this affirmation a reality, is a farce" (1970, p. 50). We don't claim to succeed in bringing engaging challenges to every class we teach. Or even to most classes. But we see glimpses of decolonizing moments of epiphany every now and then, moments when together, teachers and students, we can see the unmistakable connections between the biographical and the historical (Denzin & Giardina, 2013), between the personal trouble and the public issue (Mills, 1959), between individual struggles and socio-structural forces that make the suffering possible, between divisive and uniting narratives of being in the world (Diversi & Moreira, 2009). That is when decolonizing pedagogies seem to come to life. However fleeting, these are meaningful and unique moments in life. We don't have many settings where critical inquiry trained on the neoliberal world order can take place, in larger collectives, beyond classrooms and scholarship and politically informed activism and art. These are sites, we think, where decolonizing inquiry can introduce young and old to unifying narratives of humanity, to a sociological imagination bathed in love and respect for one another, beyond borders of all types, beyond the neoliberal narrative where the only worthwhile way of moving forward is to embrace a system that privileges few at the hard cost of many. Everyone will rise when the rich get richer, toots the neoliberal narrative machine. The classroom can be a place where these preconceived "truths" can be examined, challenged, and transformed into the larger truth that we are all here, 7 billion of us plus everyone and everything else on our planet, together. We rise together or we shall fall.

In the classroom, we can examine, challenge, and expand
Notions of
Us over Them
The role of American military in the world
From the perspective of the "helped"
The invaded
The conquered
The struck
By signature drones
For being
The Other
In the classroom, we can examine, challenge, and expand
The ways we treat
Veterans of imperial wars
Their families
The ambiguities in celebrating Memorial Day
Moving only to those who believe
That the Other's child is less
Beautiful
Than their own

We can aim to speak truth to power (Said, 1978) and in the process, inspire students to do the same, on their own terms, grounded in their own positionality and lived experience, yet always seeking a decolonizing utopia, a place we may never get to, but nonetheless a place worth wishing for.

We are aware that the nozzle around political and inclusive intellectualism is tightening. To us, it seems like it's always been the case. We feel it. Public education has been sacked. We feel it when we are asked, and threatened, to do more with less. We feel it when legislatures across the country continue to slash and burn education at all levels. We feel it when our students tell us about the size of their loans and the uncertain prospects for a living wage after graduation. We feel it when the system of tenure and promotion in higher education puts forth an increasingly mad pace for quantity of publications and citations, over quality and liberatory inclinations. We feel it when good people in our classes believe that invading countries is a compassionate act. We feel it when the good people in our classes seem comfortably numbed by the topic of drones and the unavoidable stories of innocent deaths that follow their "signature strikes."

Yet, we also feel the power of possibilities in the classroom. It is a place we can bring manifestations of hope from all walks of life. Music brings many of us together to imaginary places.

> "Why can't we give ourselves one more chance?"
> Stop the droning
> "Why can't we give this world a fair chance?"
> Stop the innocent killing
> "Why can't we give love?"
> Where is *democracy* in pre-emptive strikes?
> "Give love"
> Find a way
> "Give love"
> Let us find ways
> "Cuz love is just an old-fashioned word"
> Persistent against all odds
> "And that dares you to care for"
> All
> "The people"
> The peoples
> "On the edge of the night"
> On the edge of anywhere safe
> "And that dares you to change"
> Transform
> "Our way of caring about ourselves"
> Us without a need for Them

> "This is our last dance"
> Yet
> "This is our last chance
> This is ourselves"
>> (Eddie Vedder & Ben Harper, 2013, singing Under Pressure, by Queen, as seen on YouTube: www.youtube.com/watch?v=2NEUic49Q8c)

As liberal arts education comes, ever more, under bloody attack, we feel it.

But there is hope. Hope has to be there, here, everywhere in-between and beyond. We agree with Paulo Freire that "hope is an ontological need" (Freire, 1995/2004, p. 8). Like Freire, we can't imagine "human existence, and the struggle needed to improve it, apart from hope and dream" (p. 8). Teachers, parents, siblings, relatives, friends, peers, neighbors, concerned folks can all bring humanistic narratives to children and each other every day, to every encounter we have on a daily basis, to cafes and street corners, to art and social media, to classrooms everywhere. "How many hours of your/our life have you spent inside academic institutions?" we ask students and colleagues alike. "How has this artificial division of reality become so rooted in your/our beliefs?"

The classroom is a concrete and constant part of our lives. It is the physical and imaginary space for our pedagogy. It is in the decolonizing classroom that we seek to create space for more inclusive ways of being in and knowing the world. To us, the decolonizing classroom is a territory where struggle against oppression and dehumanization moves from memory to the classroom in the endless making of renewed narratives of resistance, transformation, and inclusiveness. We see it as a public performance stage that attempts to move us from decolonizing discourse toward decolonizing praxis, toward a community space where people come to join the talking, not just be asked to do the answering. We try to make the decolonizing classroom a place of peaceful revolution, where the oppressed and their marked bodies invade the institutional space not as *objects* of research but as *experts* of their own struggle.

It is in the decolonizing classroom that we attempt to create and show possibilities of hope, of as many versions of a decolonizing utopia as we know. It is in the classroom that we are all pushed to understand how to navigate the complex narratives of our globalized neoliberal world order. It is there that we show that we cannot understand immigration separately from the history of international trade. "No, it is not just the 'American way of life' that keeps a large number of people coming to the USA," we say to our students, "the pull is, in great part, due to the deprivation that the European and the American imperial projects (Chomsky, 2005) have brought to Latin American, African, and Asian countries." Does it not make sense? Was it not you who subjugated the Other we speak of? Let's then, here in the classroom, examine immigration from a counter-narrative of migration from the perspective of the colonized, exploited, mined, patronized, and of those in-between. We aren't aiming for a consensus, of our own preference or otherwise, but for a chance to move beyond the neoliberal narratives of self-righteousness, for a place where "progressive counter-narratives" inspire students and educators to act toward a future "where the common good triumphs over self-interest" (Goodall, 2010, p. 169).

It is there, in the decolonizing classroom, that we make the connections between our bodies – teachers and students – with the ever cruel commoditization of our cultures, lives, schools and universities, wars, and racial politics. It is there that we try to make, for example, the labor process visible, examining the fact that the neoliberal system hangs on the shoulders of women and children of color, who compose the majority of the poorly paid workers who make the goods we are all wearing in the classroom. Aisha Durham (2010) reminds us that many of our university desks and chairs are made by bodies in prisons, and that those bodies are not white. And that they are punished more harshly than their white counterparts for the very same drug possession offense.

We seek to show our students that
We are *all* responsible for the oppression
Nobody can be neutral (Zinn, 1980/2005)
And that we, the teachers, cannot let any of *us* off the hook.

★★★

Both of us work at land-grant universities whose mission is to serve the state they belong, and beyond. Chancellors talk about the importance of developing partnerships with their communities. We must take advantage of this public commitment, however neoliberalized it may be in the current times of public education starvation, and bring decolonizing narratives and critiques to this large round-table, where academics, students, and community stakeholders sit together. Again and again, we aim for a middle ground where we find ourselves on the same boat, as betweeners and border-crossing agents striving for a living, for us and ours, and therein lies the crux, with less suffering and more kindness. Our universities may be mostly populated by the privileged, but we also have a good number of students who come from the wrong side of the tracks. We seek to make our offices and classrooms into decolonizing spaces for all, but we dedicate special attention to students from the margins. Oppressed communities are not easily contained by the structures of power, and the acknowledgment of these missing bodies in our academic settings (Moreira and Diversi, 2011), as teachers and students, helps to deconstruct the dehumanizing identities of such communities. As we wrote before:

> Teach what is not supposed to be taught. Dare to teach all your students but have a special care with the ones that aren't supposed to be there… These are our New Battlegrounds. We live the struggle in so many layers.
> *(Diversi & Moreira, 2009, p. 210)*

The decolonizing classroom is part of the so-called real world. "History is still on the move. What are you waiting for? Go out, and change the world" (Denzin and Giardina, 2013, p. 22).

The decolonizing classroom is a place where we can change the world. We, teachers, decolonizing intellectuals of all stripes, must *be* hope, not the farce against which Paulo Freire (1970) warned educators even before the takeover of neoliberalism. To do so, we must make our classrooms and texts and performances sites of humanizing hope, a place that "enables transgressions – a movement against and beyond boundaries... which makes education the practice of freedom" (hooks, 1994b, p. 12). We must engage students and colleagues in examining the past critically in order to understand the present outside of and beyond the neo-liberal narrative of inevitability (i.e., there is no superior alternative to the status quo, everything else has failed, economic trickle-down is the best humanity can do, governments are to serve corporations not ordinary people). Only then can we imagine a future where critically informed citizens, able to spot the Us/Them propaganda embedded in narratives designed to maintain the neoliberal status quo, will use the democratic power of voting, of the freedom of expression and peaceful assembly guaranteed by the First Amendment, of education beyond the dominant narratives of neoliberalism, to move us toward a system where *people* and the *planet* in which we live will always come *before profit*.

It is slow moving.

But it is imperative that we continue to try.

Decolonizing Constructions of Childhood and History

511 anos depois, e os Bandeirantes continuam a pilhagem contra os indigenas e ecologia que aqui os receberam...

511 years later, and the Conquistadores keep on pillaging the indigenous people and ecology that welcomed their arrival...

★★★

History class, 3rd grade, Liceu Pasteur, expensive private school, São Paulo, Brazil, circa 1976.

"And so, after a long and perilous voyage, Pedro Alvarez Cabral discovers Brazil," Dona Teresinha says with a big smile.

She seems proud of the beginning of her country. The whole point of the lesson seems to be to make us proud with her.

"But what about the Indians?" I ask.[2]

"Raise your hand before you ask a question, Marcelo," Dona Teresinha says looking at me.

I raise my hand timidly. Dona Teresinha nods and I ask the question again.

"They welcomed the Portuguese," she says.

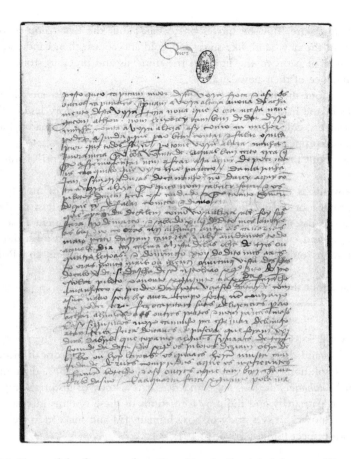

FIGURE 5.1 Copy of the first page from Pero Vaz de Caminha's letter to King Manuel I of Portugal, signed May 1, 1500, detailing his first arrival in the new land and encounter with its indigenous inhabitants. The letter reads "Eram pardos, todos nus, sem coisa alguma que lhes cobrisse suas vergonhas. Nas mãos traziam arcos com suas setas. Vinham todos rijamente sobre o bater; e Nicolau Coelho lhes fez sinal que pousassem os arcos. E eles os pousaram." (*They were dark-skinned, all naked, without any covering for their shame. They carried bows and arrows in their hands. They came tensely toward the shore; and Nicolau Coelho made a sign for them to put down their bows. And they put them down*)

Source: Pero Vaz de Caminha,[1] Thursday morning, April 23, 1500; the approximate translation is ours; from Corografia brazílica, ou relação histórico-geográfica do reino do Brazil. Composta e dedicada a sua Magestade Fidelíssima pelo presbítero Manuel Aires de Casal. Rio de Janeiro: Impressão Régia, 1817, vol. 1, pp. 12–34

I wait for more. But she moves on to talk about the first colonies, the great resources of the new land, like sugar and gold and cocoa, then bandeirantes[3] and the opening of paths to the interior, the minerals and precious stones, the lush and abundance of their new land.

"What about the Indians?" I want to ask again. There were people living in the paths of the bandeirantes. But she isn't stopping her history lesson. She talks about pioneers, colonizers, slaves, missionaries, Jesus people, monarchy, and wars with other European conquistadores.

"What about the people who lived here before the discovery?" I still want to know.

By now she is already impressing upon us the importance of memorizing the linear timeline of events, the names of European heroes, the gist of their conquests, more dates lost in time. We will learn about the present in a different class, moral and civic education, I'm told. History is the story of a distant past, relevant to us only in bits and pieces of memorized numbers and Portuguese names.

"What about the Indians?" I still want to know.

★★★

To unravel the story of research ethics with human subjects, teachers and students must understand that research ethics is not just a body of historical 'hiccups' and their legal solutions. It is a study of how societies, institutions, disciplines, and individuals *authorize, describe, settle*, and *rule*. It is a study of historical imperialism, racism, and patriarchy and the new formations of these systems in contemporary relations of power. It is a study of how humans fail and succeed at treating each other with respect (Smith, 2005, p. 101).

★★★

THIS IS A MESSY VISCERAL TEXT
   WRITTEN IN DESPAIR AND DESPERATION
   WE ASK YOU TO MEET US
   HALF-WAY BETWEEN HELL AND NARRATIVES
   BETWEEN BEING HUMAN AND THE POLITICS
   OF REPRESENTATION IN THESE DAYS OF
   GLOBALIZATION
   GLOBALIZATION
   GLOBALIZATION
   THE MODERN FACE OF COLONIZATION

And yes, representation does matter. Stuart Hall (1997) reminds us that people are treated the way they are represented. As producers of knowledge, we cannot ignore the role research has in the colonization process. The opening quote from the first European man in the land that would be called Brasil can and should also be read as the first anthropological writing of the ironic place named the "New World."

This desperation comes from living, laboring, and writing from "the tricky ground" (Smith, 2005), from the spaces in-between, Anzaldúa's borderlands, "the spaces between research methodologies, ethical principles, institutional regulations, and human subjects as individuals and as socially organized actors and communities" (Smith, 2005, p. 85). Lost in our nervousness and suffering a decolonizing call we make and we believe in Smith's powerful and wise words that

> The decolonization project in research engages in multiple layers of struggle across multiple sites... Research is not just a highly moral and civilized search for knowledge; it is a set of very human activities that reproduce particular social relations of power. Decolonizing research, then, is not about simply challenging or making refinements to qualitative research. It is... transforming the institution of research, the deep underlying structures and taken-for-granted ways of organizing, conducting, and disseminating research and knowledge. To borrow from Edward Said (1978), research can also be described as "a corporate institution" that has made statements about indigenous peoples, "authorizing views" of us, "describing [us], teaching about [us], settling [us] and ruling over [us]." It is the corporate institution of research, as well as the epistemological foundations from which it springs, that needs to be decolonized.
>
> (p. 88)

And so, lost, we ask: What is there for us? How to do it? We offer our lives as a source (Dimitriadis & McCarthy, 2000). Throughout the messy layered pages of this manuscript we insert our own biography, our bodies in history, our sociological imagination (Mills, 1959), to "cut paths in and through the determined spaces of the structures and cultures in which individuals are located" (Clarke, Hall, Jefferson, & Roberts, 2006, p. 57) with the intention to construct marginalized counter-narratives of resistance.

Constructions of (De)Colonizing Childhoods

Starting with how we teach our children about inequalities, history, its many untold stories about injustice. From where we stand, we see constructions of childhood so narrowly defined around a white middle-class adult longing for innocence that we prevent most of our children from having an age-appropriate language to make sense of the world they inhabit. We believe we should have a polyvocal story at hand, well articulated and with the intent to lead children toward conscientização (Freire, 1970), when our children ask about what happened to the Indians when the Portuguese arrived in their land. We don't have a formula for this polyvocal story, as each person who educates and cares for children will have her/his own knowledge on how to teach about inequalities. What we are trying to advance here is a paradigm shift in our constructions of childhood – from the unease about inequalities of adults identified with their dominant ethnic and/or racial group to the innate need to know about social injustice of children. We believe we can guide children toward more critical forms of citizenship by addressing social injustice head on, overtly, frankly, carefully. We believe this can help children in poverty, drowning in discrimination, violence, suffering in their own ahistorical lives. The typical response and narratives of avoidance, historical and personal detachment, and sugarcoating to social injustice only teaches children to see the Other with avoidance, historical and personal detachment, and sugarcoating.

Instead, we can teach children about perspective, the power and politics of storytelling, and the connection between personal life and history by more openly addressing the first questions about inequalities. Even when a mother doesn't know how to explain what happened to the Indians, she can avoid uncomfortable avoidance and engage in curious perspective-taking with her child. Let's seek information about that time of "discovery" and then take turns imagining varied scenarios together. Let's look at representations of that first encounter between indigenous people and European settlers and question the positionality and motives of the authors together. Let's connect, together, the dots between the "discovery" of Brazil and the inequalities that our children begin to point out in the present.

Addressing our children's questions about inequalities is more than simply sharing mundane imaginations and anecdotes about oppressed folk. Again, Stuart Hall explains positions of marginality as having budding empowerment because it

> is not simply the opening within the dominant spaces that those outside it can occupy. It is also the result of the cultural politics of difference, of the struggles around difference, of the production of new identities, of the appearance of new subjects on the political and cultural stage. This is true not only in regard to race, but also for other marginalized ethnicities, as well as around feminism and around sexual politics in the gay and lesbian movement, as a result of a new kind of cultural politics.
>
> (Hall, 1996, p. 467)

In this sense, we try to craft in this book a space that is performative (Butler, 1993; Denzin 2003; Pollock, 1998a, 1998b, 1998c) because it needs a (possible, active, and present) body that makes inscriptions in the cracks of history.

Our bodies! Emma Perez (1999) refers to this as the interstitial space in history (in the borderlands), wherein "the unspoken and unseen" reside. She asserts that it is in these interstitial breaches that oppositional and subaltern yarns can be found. Furthermore, Perez teaches us that this space "eludes invasion, a world unseen that cannot, will not, be colonized" (1999, p. 115). She adds that when heard "these silences become the negotiating spaces for the decolonized subject. Perez names it "the decolonial imaginary" (1999, p. 5). Denzin (2003) calls it performativity, the place where the doing and done collide. The performativity exists in the tension between the doing (body) and the done (text), the performance (p. 10).

Our point here is that theories of decolonization are indeed performative, and so are our collective messy stories. These theories are generated by bodies, people's lives, in these liminal and interstitial spaces, and can be reckoned with by acknowledging the possibility of performance (Madison, 1998) being understood as the relationship between history (historicity) and the body. As Della Pollock (1998b) points out, in historicity the body practices history,

> It incarnates, mediates, and resists the metahistories with which it is impressed. It wrestles with the totalizing and legitimizing power of such historical tropes as telos and progress. The body in action makes history answer to the contingencies and particularities... of everyday life.
>
> *(p. 4)*

Pollock (1998b) goes on to say that these clashes in-between historicities and among emerging different bodies are performative: "They are sites of creative practice and imaginative play. They are slippery, liminal phases, fertile with possibility of both reviewing and revising history" (p. 5).

Hence in our autoethnographic performances, what we try to do, as Pollock (1998b) emphasizes, is the embodiment of the meaning-making process in a historical moment, it "becomes the everyday practice of doing what's done" (p. 43) and is, "uniquely centered in the body and decentered by its excesses" (p. 8) where it overflows its borders and marks other performances most often changeably because "performativity is what happens when history/textuality sees itself in the mirror – and suddenly sees double; it is the disorienting, [the] disruptive" (p. 43).

Inspired once more by Della Pollock, our "disruptive act" is our attempt to advance performative writing that can be heard by children and their caring adults. Pollock (1998a, 1998b) connects the act of writing with embodied scholarship, with the body typing the words, delineating possibilities for performative writing as *evocative, metonymic, subjective, nervous, citational*, and *consequential* (1998c, pp. 80–96). Avoiding linearity in time and space, not showing the whole story at once, asking the reader to go to the next page. Before providing a more comprehensive story. We yearn for a nervous writing. Nervous not because it may include feelings of anger, compassion, suffering, or even the total amount of our emotions; nervous not

> in the sense of glancing or superficial (or even merely anxious) [but] "nervous" writing follows the body's model: it operates by synaptic relay,

drawing one charged moment into another, constituting knowledge in an ongoing process of transmission and referral, finding in the wide-ranging play of textuality an urgency that keeps what amounts to textual travel from lapsing into tourism, and that binds the traveler to his/her surging course like an electrical charge to its conduit.

(Pollock, 1998c, p. 91)

The same nervous(ness) we find in our travels to multiple pasts in quest of memories, and the bleak present we live in.

The same nervousness we find in the stories we thought we would write and the ones we actually write.

The same nervousness we find in our conflicting messy lives that leads us to conclude by asking: How in the world can writing about people *not* be messy?

Through the apparent disconnection between bodies, history, and stories we present here, we attempt to create our "disruptive" cracks, where we invite you the reader to insert your own body and life's story in the hope that our desperation may move you into action!

HALF-WAY BETWEEN HELL AND NARRATIVES

511 years is a long time and the future does not look that promising!

The horror of that time continues to distort our ideals of equality!

How does one interrupt THAT?

★★★

Her hand quickly covered my eyes. But at 5 years of age, I need to look again at what I've just seen. On her lap, I wiggle out of her grasp just enough to see again the naked little kids walking about a dirt patch next to the paved road. She let me be. As we continue to drive westward, I see the naked little kids fade away through the right-side window.

"Who is going to take care of those little kids?" I ask my mom.

"Their parents take care of them, honey," she says with a little smile and looking kindly into my eyes.

"But they were alone. Side of the road. Many cars driving fast," I insist.

I don't remember what my mom said next. But I assume it didn't make sense to me at the time. How could a mother explain to her 5-year-old child who sleeps in a comfortable bed, eats an abundance of the healthiest food, has a playground in the backyard, and is driven around everywhere that most children out there don't enjoy the same fortune?

How does a mother of a young child answer the first questions of injustice?

The child is trying to make sense of the world

It may be rudimentary at this early stage

But the realization of deep inequalities becomes obvious at some point

In every child's life

Explanations are needed
Stories are told
And what grand stories we tell!
Stories of superiority
Stories of Us and Them
Rationalized tribal stories
Stories of civilization
Stories of Christianity
(Middle) Finger pointing
From a higher moral horse
Subjugating those who lost
Or simply chose
Not to take the best meat[4]

Again, where does a mother start to explain inequalities to her young child? Industrial revolution? Agricultural encroachment? Rural exodus? The promise and the horror of the big city? Migration away from kin? Colonization? 300 years of slavery? Indigenous genocide? How deep does a mother's memories have to go in history to tell the story of inequalities? Memories that deep have to come from (hi)stories larger and much older than the individual mother.

A mother tells the (hi)stories at hand.

★★★

I am now sitting at home, around 6 pm on a Tuesday, taking a break from several hours of writing and thinking about "constructions of childhood" and its connection with social inequalities in Brazil, enraged that Lula, the Workers' Party, and now our presidenta guerrilheira, Dilma, have pushed the Belo Monte Dam in the Xingu River through legislation, bribery, and the ultimate destruction of many of the last indigenous peoples of South America. I've been sick to my stomach since this final step was announced on May 31. Have you seen the image of Chief Raoni crying as he heard the news that Dilma had signed the final approval for the dam construction to begin? Some say it's a much older picture inserted out of context to make for a more compelling story, and that Chief Raoni instead of crying vowed to fight to the end against the Belo Monte Monster Dam. Either way the image is fitting.

How could Lula and Dilma do this to the indigenous people of the Xingu River?! I would expect the usual suspects to do this. But not Lula and Dilma. They have fought so hard for more dignity and emancipation among our poorest and social outcasts. They've experienced colonizing oppression first hand. Their bodies have been marked by it. They've choked up in the most genuine ways when confronted with the brutal injustices of our history.

How, then, could they not see what they are doing to thousands of people from many indigenous ethnicities along the Xingu River?! How could they not

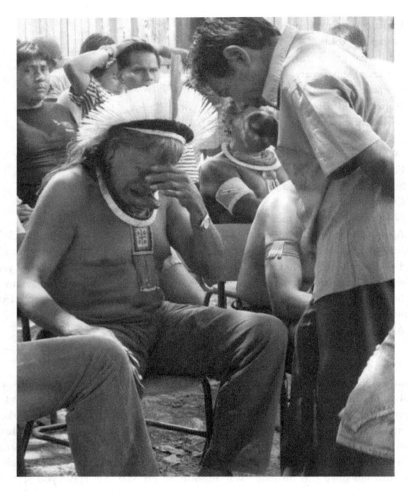

FIGURE 5.2 Chief Raoni
Note: This picture was freely shared by www.facebook.com/pages/Support-Chief-Raoni/206875702683503

see that they are the leaders of the final act of a cultural genocide that started when the first Europeans arrived in Bahia more than 500 years ago?! And to commit this brutality for a few kilowatts of electricity?! This is only possible because Lula and Dilma can't see the Caiapos as fully human, as equals, as brothers and sisters who, like them, want to live a just and dignified life in their original land.

I can't imagine other more likely explanations, as much as I have tried to in the last few weeks. If they saw the indigenous peoples of the Amazon as fellow human beings, they would never support a plan that involves up to 60 dams all over the western Amazon rivers that will effectively complete the colonizing project of taking over the land at whatever cost to the indigenous peoples – pesky and stubborn obstacles that continue to delay the final conquest toward total European supremacy of the Americas. But no, Lula and Dilma cry only for their "civilized" sisters and brothers in arms. Dilma proclaimed in her inauguration speech that she would be the president of all Brazilians, working for justice, equality, dignity for all fellow country people.

An urge to yell: "But how can a dam that floods ancient civilizations be justice?"

There is no justice in bringing concrete, bulldozers, steel, disease, deforestation, massive flooding, and ultimate homeland displacement to thousands of indigenous groups. No, indigenous peoples are not equal to Dilma, not her brothers and sisters, not her fellow Brazilians, not part of "all Brazilians." It's like witnessing the first arrival of Europeans all over again, fully cognizant that I will be a useless and helpless observer of a modern genocide of historical proportions. Damn that part of our humanity!

★★★

Is there a history book with my story?

Or is my history nothing more than an extra amount of collecting anecdotes always dismissed by the official storytellers?

Is there a book out there for me? About my tale of violence?

Violence

Once upon a time in a faraway land I came up with an idea to make a little money. I was 10 or so. It was right before I started to work at Trimag. I talked Grandma into it. She would make some juice and put it in small plastic bags, and then freeze the bags. Using a cooler, I'd sell the bags in the streets. Nothing new here. These little bags of frozen juice were known as "laranjinhas" or "chup-chups." They were the cheap version of Popsicle. The novelty was that I would work on my own for the first time.

After two or three days, I realized that my business wasn't going well. I gave many of my bags away for free to friends of mine who, like me, had little money. So I devised a new plan. I was going to sell my stuff downtown. Lots of people with money there, I thought, and no friends. I knew how to put on a wretched face so people would feel compelled to help a poor kid.

That was my routine during vacation from school. I would leave the hood very early and quietly. Didn't want to be seen by my friends. I was learning to be greedy. I wanted the money.

One day, turning the corner as I walk to the bus stop, I bump into Joao Henrique. Joao Henrique is a real mean guy. And worse, a much older and strong mean guy. I am scared. There is no place to run. Looking at me, Joao Henrique says:

"Give me one."

I do.

With a smile, he goes on,

"This tastes like crap. Give me another."

I did.

"This is shit."

Gathering courage, I try to talk back. It comes like a whisper from my mouth, "You owe me 50 cents."

Joao Henrique moves and takes the cooler away from me. I am very scared.

"How dare you. You want me to pay for this shit?" Looking inside the cooler, he says: "Let's see the flavors you have." Joao Henrique takes another of my laranjinhas. The smile always on his face.

"Much better. This tastes like your sister's pussy. The rest is crap." Then, Joao Henrique throws everything onto the pavement.

I am crying now.

"Motherfucker!" I yell at him already regretting what I just did.

Joao Henrique comes strong toward me. He punches me in the face. I fall to the ground. There is blood coming from my nose. I am in pain. I am crying and yelling:

"Fucking motherfucker."

Joao Henrique kicks me in the ribs. I can't breathe. He then opens his zipper and starts peeing on me. I try to crawl. Can't do shit… Then, Joao Henrique starts running away.

I don't understand…

Then, I see Roni, my friend, and his older brother Eddy. Now, I know why Joao Henrique ran. Eddy is the baddest ass in the hood.

Roni is crying too. Eddy grabs my hand and says:

"Hey kid, I'm gonna get him for this."

And he did.

★★★

Bom, to aqui todo destruido emocionalmente com a estoria da Belo Monte Dam no Rio Xingu…voce viu a imagem do Raoni (Chief dos Caiapos e parte das minhas primeiras memorias sobre a colonizacao do brasil) chorando ao receber noticia de que a Dilma tinha aprovado a construcao da Belo Monte? Se nao viu, don't go looking for it. It's too heartbreaking and you don't need any more of that now. Soh queria te dizer o que ta acontecendo aqui na minha vida. nao to conseguindo engolir a traicao da dilma e do PT. Demorou 511 anos, mas a conquista total do velho oeste brasileiro eh assinada pela nossa presidenta guerrilheira. Me senti como o braveheart no campo de batalha quando descobre que o "final blow" vem pela traicao do principe escoces.

Tentando ter coragem…[5]

★★★

Tentando ter coragem…
511 years without history! How are my stories connected with genocide? How a
History of a fairly white child is viscerally connected with elder Raoni, Lula, Brother Marcelo, guerrilla president, Custer and Denzin?
Wasn't Dilma part of the Araguaia guerrilla[6] in the Amazon region known as Xambioa?
Am I caboclo?[7]
Can I refuse the matuto?[8]
The crossroad of lives and absence of history
I must be crazy because it is only a

Tooth

Let me tell you this. I was 12 or 13, whatever. I lost a tooth in a fight. It wasn't a fight… I just got the shit kicked out of me.

It wasn't a front tooth, it was a molar.

Do you have an idea how bad you need to get beat to lose a molar?

These motherfuckers don't just fall off. And my molar did not fall off, it was kinda loose.

I was in bad shape. Grandma took me to the ER, the one in the Med School that accepted poor people. There, the doctors told us that since the tooth was loose and I have a big cavity on it, I would be better off without it. So, the doctor or the dentist finished the job.

Years later, when I was on my way to becoming a middle-class guy, I went to the dentist. She asked me about my tooth, the empty space I have. I told her.

My dentist then told me that what they did to me was a crime. You don't take a molar out. Some of the problems I have in my mouth are due to that empty space.

The difference?

This time I was paying the bill. But this is not my only point.

For more than 20 years, every time I have felt threatened, my tongue touches that empty space… and please… no psychology here. The list can go on and on. And I am aware that I was not the only one. Not only this, I've met and seen people who got way worse than I did and … oppression is marked on my body.

The scars are part of how I am, not only who I am.

★★★

Email to a friend on June 8, 2011

> ps: on a related note, i wanted to say that i devoured your Custer on Canvas this past week! very powerful way of presenting non-conquerors' stories

about Custer, the seventh cavalry, and the larger mythology of the benign "founding fathers" and the "birth" of the American democracy and freedom. to me, you have painted a "new masterpiece" of Custer, the Last Stand, the brutal colonization of north america, of all americas, of the world. and once again you have given me hope and representations to imagine "a world without end," without Last Stands, a new beginning. and for that, i am forever grateful to you. i've been doing existential battle with the recent development in Brazil, in the heart of the Amazon, where our newly elected guerilla president, from the worker's party, a heroine of mine because of her freedom fighting battle against the military regime in the 60's and 70's, my "presidente guerrilheira," who moved me so during her acceptance speech and her inauguration words of "a new beginning, a renewed commitment to social justice," has just approved the construction of the Belo Monte Dam. Chief Raoni, an elder i've followed since my own childhood, the chief from the Kayapo tribe, wept a few days back, on May 31 to be exact, in front of his family, tribe, and international journalists when he heard that our freedom fighter president Dilma Rousseff signed the final approval for the hydroelectric plant to start construction to dam the Xingu River. Here is a short video from Amazon Watch in case you have 3 minutes and interest to have a glimpse into this contemporary genocide, tragically, as usual, framed as inevitable modernization, our modern narrative of colonization: http://amazonwatch.org/take-action/stop-the-belo-monte-monster-dam

    this is their Last Stand. it's about to happen and i can't stop wondering what to do. in a way, to me, especially after just having read Custer on Canvas, it's like going back to the early days of june, 1876, knowing that Custer and the settlers are coming, now for the Kayapo, Juruna, Enawene Nawe, Arara, Bororo, Xavante, Cinta Larga, Terena, Bakairi, and the Fulni-ô. in English, this has also been described in the media as The Last Stand. i'm about to witness a cultural and ecological genocide of epic proportions. 20,000 indigenous people immediately displaced. memories flooded by the thoughtless greed of the modern conquistadores. the Xingu River indigenous people will never again find their way around. and a brazilian cousin recently told me there were no longer "indios" left in Brazil. his memory of "brazilian" indians died with his history textbook. no wonder our presidente guerrilheira can sign away the lives of so many indigenous people. today i can't make myself believe in the possibility of a new beginning outside the circle of revenge. but i stay hopeful that years from now someone like you will be able to paint a new masterpiece of Chief Raoni's Last Stand, a new painting where his tears and fierceness will evoke a sadness for humanity, not simply a sadness for the Kayapo and the Xingu River peoples.

★★★

I wrote about Geraldo before!

Does history repeat itself? Or is it only us and the power enforcers that don't want to take the bone out of the jaws of Rottweiler, big dog corporations?

It does hurt.

How to use my body, bringing history and biography together

Using our sociological imagination

To fight back, to expose the Rottweiler and be dangerous to power (Madison, 2009)?

> I would argue that a *dangerous ethnography* does not begin with interventions on political economies or structures of the state or the nation, on global capitalism or corporate greed, or even on ideologies of neoliberalism or fundamentalism – these are the targets of a dangerous ethnography (with some complication) but they are not the starting point, not the inspiration. My inspiration for a dangerous ethnography begins with performance – that is, the body in the performance.
>
> *(Madison, 2009, p. 191)*

Is there a history book out there for me?

'Cause, all I have is

Memories

Two short ones.

First:

When the dark body of Grandpa Geraldo died he could not be buried because officially he was never born!

One cannot be more without history than this, eh?

Eric R. Wolf's (1982) "people without history?"

Second:

Probably one of my few memories of Geraldo, my grandfather

Like blurred images from an old movie, long watched and difficult to remember

Walking in the park in my hometown

The Po-lice approaching Geraldo

Geraldo saying to the cops: "Yes, I know. This kid here, Claudio, is pretty darn white. But he is my grandson!"

Mother running to save the day

Of course, Geraldo did not have an ID on him

But Claudio, what does the dam have to do with the beating you took from an older kid? And presidents, and the skin color of your grandfather, and Marcelo's rage?

The Belo Monte Monster Dam *is* HISTORY!

We treat history differently. We take history out of context and quote it back against itself, troubling at least the hierarchy between history and story. We are not looking for the truth, the official history, here. We are performing the past not to "recognize it the way it really was," but "to seize hold of a memory as it flashes up at a moment of danger" (Benjamin, 1968, p. 255), to embody and recreate the past, and insert it in the troubled present, not as a succession of events, but as a series of scenes, inventions, emotions, images, and stories (Ulmer, 1989). We are, right now, historicizing the body, again quoting history back to itself. In bringing memories into the public, political, pedagogical, and physical space of these pages, we are conflicting the official history of colonization with our own personal stories of race, ethnicity, and class; making it impossible to separate historical bodies playing their powerful hand in the Belo Monte Dam affair and our mundane personal lives. Thus, Marcelo's cousin statement, that there are no more Indians in Brazil, becomes unthinkable. Then it becomes unthinkable, the separation of the bodies of Dilma and Raoni. Then, it becomes unthinkable to feel connected with our fellow indigenous people... human beings like you and me... betweeners! Yes, right now we invite you, together, "to create the conditions for rewriting and hence re-experiencing it" (Denzin, 2009, p. 209) in the hope of a just future, because the other option is criminal: another government-sponsored genocide!

511 years and still counting...

Until when, we ask no one.

Until when, we ask you.

***

I am still in shock that my freedom fighter president, Dilma, gave the go ahead for a monster dam to be built in the heart of the Xingu River, one of the major tributaries of the Amazon River and millennial home to thousands of indigenous people from a dozen or so tribes, and four times more ecologically diverse than the entire European continent. It's like witnessing Che Guevara turn his people in to imperial forces... or sell Mary Kay products at your doorstep. The genocide against indigenous peoples of the world is already debilitating. But the betrayal in this case is more than I can fathom.

***

511 years later, and the conquistadores keep on pillaging the indigenous people and ecology that welcomed their arrival.

My tongue is touching the empty space inside my mouth where

A tooth used to be 'cause

The genocide against indigenous peoples of the world is already debilitating. But the betrayal in this case is more than I can handle.

Where is my fucking history?

Did you, Marcelo, study about it in your fancy, expensive, state-of-the-art private school?

Isn't Lula, me, Dilma, brothers Marcelo and Denzin, you too, viscerally related, civically responsible to the (A)History of the Matuto?

> The matutos' faces are browner; their bodies are smaller and slighter. One might see them as tough and sinewy, but that would be at variance with their own image of themselves as weak, wasted, and worn-out. One can see both the Amerindian and the African in their eyes, cheekbones, hair, and skin, although the African predominates... These people are the descendants of a slave runaway slave-Indian, caboclo, population. Yet, they do not think to link their current difficulties to a history of slavery and race exploitation... They call themselves *os pobres* (the poor), and they describe themselves as *moreno* (brown), almost never as *preto or negro* (black). They are "brown," then, as all Brazilians, rich and poor, are said to be "brown." In this way the ideology of a "racial democracy" goes unchallenged, uncontested, into another generation.
> *(Scheper-Hughes, 1992, p. 90)*

Or are we only accomplices of a "racial democracy" in Brazil and elsewhere, hoping that at the end of the day there are still enough Mary Kay products and enough electricity outlets to plug our green cars and other stuff?

And that we are the saviors of the savages?

WHAT WE THOUGHT TO WRITE AND WHAT WE ACTUALLY WRITE

Where are my roots?

> It's actually the white Anglo dominant culture that privileges the white in us, that tries to erase, to hide the fact that we have African blood, the fact that we have Indian blood, and only a very small percentage of Spanish blood.
> *(Anzaldúa, 2000, p. 181)*

Grandbrownfather!

I wrote about Geraldo before.

★★★

> I am not here to boast of my own life story, but rather to praise the life of every Brazilian woman. My greatest commitment, I repeat, is to honoring our women, protecting our most vulnerable people, and governing for everyone. I am here, above all, to carry on the greatest process of affirmation that this country has experienced in recent times.
> *(Dilma Rousseff, in her acceptance speech as the first woman president of Brazil, November 2, 2010)*

And the children will continue to ask, "What happened to the Indians?"

Notes

1 Pero Vaz de Caminha was a Portuguese nobleman in charge of documenting the voyage for the King of Portugal. In a long letter, he describes the very first encounter with the indigenous people in diary form. The entry above is the very first description he writes about the encounter.
2 Michael Yellow Bird (2004) argues that the terms Indian and Native American are terms defined by the European conquerors. Like him, we prefer the terms First Nations or indigenous peoples.
3 Bandeirantes (flag bearers) are the Portuguese equivalent of the more well-known Spanish conquistadores. The bandeirantes were experienced military commanders with a sense of adventure, charged by the King of Portugal with searching for precious stones, gold, silver, hardwood, indigenous tribes, and exotic animal inland. They opened trails linking the coast with inland goods and were central to the early human traffic of enslaved natives and Africans. Current history textbooks still describe the Bandeirantes largely as brave pioneers and heroes (Taunay, 1975; Fausto, 1996). The most modern and admired highway in the state of São Paulo is named Bandeirantes. Parks, oversized monuments, neighborhoods, and key avenues in the city of São Paulo are named after them. All is festive celebration. Still.
4 We borrow this expression from Aaron Huey's (2010) explanation of the Lakota word for a non-indigenous person, "wasichu," the one who takes the best meat without regard for others.
5 We debated about whether to translate this passage. But we agreed that a more curious reader may have access to easy and free online translation. The shortcut is that this passage is a short composite of our reactions to the approval of the Belo Monte Monster Dam already shared in English. We hope you don't mind the inconvenience.
6 The Araguaia guerrilla was an armed movement against the military dictatorship of Brazil, active from 1966 to 1974 in the Araguaia river banks.
7 A copper-colored, 'civilized,' or mestizo Indian, person of mixed and white ancestry.
8 One who comes from the mato (bush, jungle, forest); rustic country person.

PART III

Contemporary Issues on Us versus Them

6
BETWEENER AUTOETHNOGRAPHIES

From different moments throughout our professional careers, we have come together to write our biographies into history (Mills, 1959), creating stories that at the same time resist and demand to be told, moving from personal troubles to public issues, refusing hegemonic pictures of reality through reductionist methodologies and pedagogies, where oppressed bodies and lived experiences are missing, or (mis)represented as exotic, deviant, decontextualized, glorified. Like many others, before and with us, we write autoethnography together to bring personal troubles to living history with the intent of disrupting essentializing representations and interpretations of lived experience. The words of Bryant Keith Alexander, then, become very important to us,

> Issues of personal survival motivate scholarship production... I am exploring and sometimes exposing my own vulnerability to racial, gender, and cultural critique as a method of both understanding self and other, self as other, while engaging in performances (written and embodied) that seek to transform the social and cultural conditions under which I live and labor.
>
> *(2005, p. 433)*

Like him, we write with the hope that we will invite historically marginalized outcasts into conversations about decolonizing knowledge production in academia. We write against repeated exclusionary treatment of the Other from our own biographies and political bodies.

Our autoethnography, to be sure, is no better than many other versions we read in scholarly texts, or hear and feel in classrooms and professional conferences. Yet it is singular in that it comes out of a deep and long friendship, marked by the usual joys and shared experiences, and by a particular shared concern with the brutal inequalities we witnessed while growing up in Brazil. We were not innocent bystanders, of course. As we see it, no one is an innocent bystander in their own times. Growing up as white heterosexual males located us as co-constructing agents of the brutal inequalities that so troubled us as children and then young men, even if our participation in the making of our social worlds was somewhat indirect to the making of the systems of oppression and domination around us. Our friendship also made us powerfully aware of our own social class differences. And we are enormously grateful that we, somehow, at the height of our late teen years and idealism, managed to lean on our immediate and magnetic affinity to find ways around the structural divides of class, classism, and everyday life. In the process of leaning on each other in search of hope for a less brutally unequal future, we followed similar educational and professional paths, all the while staying entangled in our youthful ideals to do what we can to advance Paulo Freire's pedagogy of hope (Freire, 1995/2004). And so, we lean on his pedagogy of hope ever more,

> while I certainly cannot ignore hopelessness as a concrete entity, nor turn a blind eye to the historical, economic, and social reasons that explain that hopelessness, I do not understand human existence, and the struggle needed to improve it, apart from hope and dream. Hope is an ontological need. Hopelessness is but hope that has lost its bearings, and become a distortion of that ontological need.
>
> (p. 8)

Since joining each other in scholarship and profession, we have been bound by a commitment to ground the political back on the body, on the actual *backs* that reflect back the politics of exclusion of our times. We want our autoethnography to work as a magnifying glass on this reflection, the reflection that each body sends back to the relational world we live in. We want our autoethnography to examine, deconstruct, and trouble the reflection that each of our own bodies sends back to the intersections of race, gender, sexuality, nationality, and class shaping and informing our encounters with students, scholarly texts, and the politics of knowledge production.

To us, autoethnography is a slippery concept that escapes rigid definitions and easy categorizations. Autoethnography emerged out of the clash between social sciences, humanities, and the arts. Autoethnography happens when the performance and performativity collide, in the moment of the performance, in the researcher's body as it interacts with the world, with others, with the Other, as it is reflected onto the Other by his/her research representations.

Why do we autoethnographically write?

To place ourselves in history so it doesn't go behind our backs

To perform solidarity

To perform community

To perform social justice
To all and not only to those who look like us
Or believe in what we believe
Inclusionary social justice or bust
And so We perform
The volatile
The mundane
The human
And so We perform
An ontological turn
Toward a being that is always political
Always writing from the visceral
Experience of everyday life
Of the body
And so We perform
An epistemological (re)turn
To Sartre's *universal singular* and *singular universal*
To C. W. Mills' *sociological imagination*
To Freire's *conscientização*
To Anzaldúa's *nepantlera*
To our *betweener* dialogue

Autoethnography came to us out of the poststructuralist movement of the 1980s and 1990s in the American humanities and social sciences, out of the crisis of representation (Clifford & Marcus, 1986; Denzin & Lincoln, 1994; Turner & Bruner, 1986). Within the field of performance studies, autoethnography is situated in the intersections of Third World feminism, postcolonialism, cultural studies, and critical pedagogy (Denzin, 2003; Pineau, 1998). It works to destabilize and subvert the supremacy in the dichotomies of body and mind, theory and practice, personal and political, researcher and subject so pervasive in academic settings.

We always ask, how do we write our stories? Our history? How do we write our history interlaced with the history of so many oppressed humans from so many singularities and shared universalities (Crittenden, 1998; Sartre, 1963)? So we search, over and over, for an autoethnography that is performative and transgressive, one that includes sentiments of anger, suffering, compassion, the totality of emotions we feel when confronted with brutal inequalities, with obvious injustice, with lame justifications and excuses by those with more privilege and power "to name the world" (Freire, 1970). We search for an autoethnography that refutes a superficial reading/gaze of our anxiety vis-à-vis the extreme positions of injustice we encounter every day. We search for a form of being, writing, and thinking that goes, without apology, after the structures of power that shape and maintain such systems of oppression. We search in our autoethnography an alternative model of writing, one that, like our betweener bodies, exposes the breaks and cracks of our existence in these neocolonial times. We lean on autoethnography to search for a writing that honors stories and histories of suffering bodies that, more often than not, inhabit the position of honorable subjects and not that of researchers and knowledge makers (Diversi & Moreira, 2009). We see autoethnography as a way of being and writing ourselves into the history of resistance against oppression, injustice, and exclusion, one that *starts* from our common humanity betweener identities in order to *defy* the academic preference for sophisticated Foulcaultian analysis of power and to *honor* pedestrian narratives of blood and profanity.

We want to act upon the world
As betweeners
Calling on everyone's common betweenness
By writing from the heart (Pelias, 2004)
Against ideologies of domination (hooks, 1994b)

Perhaps, we think, *betweener autoethnographies* can help us imagine a more just future for more people by helping us chip away at the powerful grip of essentialism, of determinism, of binary interpretations and representations of lived experience, of seeing the world inevitably stuck between essentializing notions of Us and Them. We think we have to get rid of essentializing views of the Other as a matter of principle, for only then can we start to realize, really, that we are all, every one of us, on the same boat. As our numbers increase exponentially, our economies become ever more intertwined, our hunger for energy grows in steady leaps, and technology makes globalization of lived experience ever more present, Our destinies, across-between-within cultures, get ever more entangled and interdependent. In the near future, we will float or sink together. So we find it imperative to return, over and over, to the basic principle of finding guidance and hope in our common humanity, in figuring out ways to write this common humanity into the forefront of pedagogy and knowledge production. In this spirit, criticism of systems of oppression and ideologies of domination needs to be grounded, in our view, on an ontological turn to our common humanity, our common challenges, our common predicaments, our common hopes.

Perhaps, we think, *betweener autoethnography* can help us find ways to critique the status quo while doing so within an ethics of caring and forgiveness, with a "good mind" (Diversi & Henhawk, 2012). When we finally see the Other, the different, including the opposition, as brothers, as sisters, violence as a means of personal gain might cease to be so prevalent. Meeting each other half-way, in the in-between spaces of Us/Them, especially when it is hardest, is the only way to move toward justice, equality, and liberty. Autoethnography, to us, is a way to create texts and performances of possibilities for a world that can find itself united in the common cause of survival, joy, and the easing of pain. We think autoethnography can be a way to co-create collective imaginations about unity and togetherness, by connecting the dots between the biographical and the historical, by moving back and forth between the personal and the political (Holman Jones,

2005), by performing this connection in classrooms and scholarship (Diversi & Moreira, 2009).

> In a performance of possibilities, moral responsibilities and artistic excellence culminate in an active intervention to break through unfair closures, remake the possibility for new openings, and bring the margins to the shared center… [It] does not arrogantly assume that we are giving voice to the silenced, for we understand that they speak and have been speaking in spaces and places often foreign to us.
>
> *(Madison, 2005, p. 178)*

> difficulty lies in the pressing need for scholars to decolonize and deconstruct those structures [of power] within the Western academy that privilege Western knowledge systems and their epistemologies… The decolonizing project reverses this equation, making Western systems of knowledge the object of inquiry.
>
> *(Denzin, 2005, p. 936)*

Betweener Autoethnography as a Decolonizing Act

Essentializing the Other has long been a colonizing strategy. Flatten the Other into a single category, a single story, and oppression can happen without much internal conflict for the oppressor. Insist on representing the Other as savage, as uncivilized, and domination follows with little resistance. One can find evidence of essentializing as a colonizing act as far back as the written word goes. European colonization of the Americas, Africa, Oceania, and Asia was deeply rooted on the notion that the Other was a monster, at best a subhuman being (for poignant examples, see Arjana, 2015; Adichie, 2009), and, thus, ready to be used and violated for their own colonizing purposes and gains. While European imperial powers did not invent colonization, much of the world today continues to be shaped by the power systems and macro-structures resulting from their 500 years of occupation, plunder, genocide, and exploitation. Indigenous peoples continue to be dislocated by the colonial impetus of occupation and economic exploitation of energy resources everywhere (Diversi, 2014; Indian Country, 2015). Decolonization, thus, continues to be a call to arms in the 21st century. As we write in our working definition earlier in this manuscript, we see our *betweener autoethnographies* as decolonizing acts, as our attempt to write ourselves into the history-in-the-making of our times. We attempt, through our betweener autoethnographies, to join the call to arms toward a decolonial imaginary (Perez, 1999), in order to examine the history of colonization as expressed in present-day bodies and systems of oppression, in order to resist current colonization of minds, bodies, and lands, and in order to offer alternative stories of being and knowing beyond the persistent Us/Them imaginary. We attempt to follow Gloria Anzaldúa's (1981, 1987/1999) footsteps and embrace the borderlands where we can all resonate with the sting of discrimination, where we can all find ways to move the world toward greater inclusion.

Yet we often find ourselves confronted by narratives of decolonization that seem to start from the very *essentialism* used in colonizing acts. Some argue that decolonization is not a metaphor and that settlers everywhere need to up and go, literally (Tuck & Yang, 2012). Some argue that decolonization can only be done by indigenous peoples (Barker, 2011). So who will determine identity here? Who are the settlers in Tuck and Yang's imagination? Who determines the *authentic* in these cases? Who gives themselves the power to essentialize the Other? Who has the moral stand to flatten betweener bodies into single identities of settlers or natives? Most of us, if not all, are hybrids and mutts of some kind or another. Indigenous peoples included. We have all been mixing up with neighbors, friends, allies, and enemies long before ideas of purity and authenticity, or *essentialism*, were first spoken.

Where would we go back to in this view of decolonization?

What part of our betweener bodies should we leave behind?

What parts should we take back to our pre-colonizing homes?

Where would all the hybrids, the hyphened, the mutts go?

How would a mass removal of people from native lands help us move forward in our global times?

How would a new ethnocide remedy previous genocides and conquering?

The issue of "authenticity" claimed by essentializing forms of decolonization has been itself one of the most powerful tools of colonization. We are capable of understanding and empathizing with any aboriginal person who would like to have the settlers, the oppressors, the colonizers leave their aboriginal lands. It seems that in some places of more recent conquest this could even happen in practical terms. But at a global level, this type of essentialist view of decolonization misses or ignores the many decades of postcolonial lived experience, scholarship, and activism (Bhabha, 1994; Denzin, 2003; Fanon, 1952/2008, 2004/1963; Freire, 1970; Said, 1978). Not to mention that, to the best of our knowledge, all aboriginal peoples were/are migrants themselves. Unless one subscribes to the idea of the noble savage, we all have to contend with a history of occupation struggle going back as far as the stories have survived.

Yes, we agree that the impatience and determination with which historically displaced peoples resist and challenge neocolonialism are central to nurturing the decolonization movement as it pushes forward against great odds. We admire and honor Tuck and Yang's quote, "We provide this framework so that we can be more impatient with each other, less likely to accept gestures and half-steps, and more willing to press for acts which unsettle innocence" (2012, p. 10). We like the idea of being more impatient with each other as we search for ontological, epistemological, and ethical turns toward decolonization. But their fixed categories of natives, slaves, and settlers do not match the decolonial imaginary of an ever more globalized existence. Most of us live, more and more, in Homi

Bhabha's third space, in transnational identities, in a postcolonial juxtaposition of mess, chaos, hybridity, and in-betweenness. Fixed identity categories of the Other misrepresent the human experience as its complexities of identities, always in the making, always in relation to others. Fixed categories of being rewrite all of us back into the Us/Them corner.

Our reading of Paulo Freire, whose pedagogy of hope continues to guide our betweener autoethnograhies and decolonizing classrooms, suggests that he would be the first to acknowledge the impossibility and futility of the search for authenticity or purity, or any other binary, either/or philosophy of being and knowing. Freire (1970) cites Fanon as he develops his ideas about how to overcome an Us/Them mentality, where subjugation is inescapable destiny, where the status quo is the way life has always been, and where the notion of change is foolish and futile. We think that Freire's philosophy has offered hope for all of us to get along, regardless of our tribal origins and fleeting allegiances.

Tuck and Yang's (2012) essentialist approach to decolonization, and they are not alone, pushes us back into a dichotomous relational system with each other that makes decolonial collaboration and cooperation impossible, even undesirable. They write,

> the settler intellectual who hybridizes decolonial thought with Western critical traditions (metaphorizing decolonization), emerges superior to both Native intellectuals and continental theorists simultaneously. With his critical hawk-eye, he again sees the critique better than anyone and sees the world from a loftier station.
>
> *(p. 16)*

As we learned from Denzin (2005, 2010), decolonization goes beyond identity politics and focuses on Western epistemologies and production of knowledge as the objects of inquiry. As Deloria (1969) taught us, invoking a notion of purity was itself a colonizing pretext of the settlers arriving in America. In grounding the call for decolonization on essentialist notions of the Other, scholars seem to reinforce the same oppression they aim to criticize. Linda T. Smith, too, echoes Deloria in the question of essentialism:

> The desire for "pure," uncontaminated, and simple definitions of the native by the settler is often a desire to continue to know and define the Other, whereas the desire by the native to be self-defining and self-naming can be read as a desire to be free, to escape definition, to be complicated, to develop and change, and to be regarded as fully human. In between such desires are multiple and shifting identities and hybridities which much more nuances positions about what constitutes native identities, native communities, and native knowledge in anti/postcolonial times.
>
> *(Smith, 2005, p. 86)*

Again, we ask, how can decolonizing essentialism help us move forward? How does decolonizing essentialism help us understand the cultural hybridity of our postcolonial times? According to decolonizing essentialism, are we settlers in the United States who should move back to Brazil, then figure out how to move back to our known and unknown ancestral lands before the European colonization of where we were born? As far as we know, we have African, Portuguese, Indigenous (unknown tribes in what is now Brazil), Italian, Scottish, and Spanish ancestry. Where do we go back to? How would Tuck and Yang's essentialist decolonization approach deal with the millions upon millions of betweeners and hybrids born on the land they want returned to native peoples? They use Frantz Fanon's work to justify an essentialist decolonization approach yet ignore the fact that he was married to a French woman, had hybrid children, wrote in the colonizer's language. They stand on Audre Lorde's shoulders yet ignore her own betweener standpoint as a Black woman born in New York City, whose ancestors were brought by Europeans as slaves from Africa to colonize Caribbean islands occupied by indigenous peoples. Decolonization needs more gray areas for all humanity to meet, not more boundaries reified by essentialist identities.

Toward Inclusive Decolonization

> Latin American representatives refused to ascribe me the standing of educator. At least I was not an educator as far as they were concerned. And they criticized me for what seemed to them to be my exaggerated "politicization." They failed to perceive that, in denying me the status of educator for being "too political," they were being as political as I. Of course, on opposite sides of the fence. "Neutral" they were not, nor could ever be.
>
> (Freire, 1995/2004, p. 7)

We find ourselves returning to Paulo Freire whenever confronted with essentialist approaches to liberation and decolonization. Freire bases his entire work on conscientization and its direct connection to systems of oppression. Conscientization is a deeply historical, cultural, and contextual approach to pedagogy and knowledge production, as it is a process of personal awareness about one's own connections with history, whereby one becomes increasingly aware of how her/his own life has been shaped and informed by larger power systems and cultural imaginations. He specifically writes about how both the oppressor and the oppressed came from the same experience of colonization in Brazil, where Europeans arrived in search of gold, precious stones, slaves, wood, and anything else that would enrich them and the European coffers, at the expense of natives, sailors, and the land. He does so fully aware that the European colonization of Brazil started almost 500 years before his own birth. That is more than 15 generations of colonial rape and subsequent mingling of people. It seems only logical that Freire is not talking about liberation as an attempt to send the Portuguese,

Dutch, English, Spanish, and French back home. He fully understands that 500 years of colonization has brought about hybridity and ethnic mixing. While the first encounters were likely violent and purely oppressive, most people of present-day Brazil are the result of loving relationships between highly mixed peoples.

The oppressed, in Freire's seminal book, *Pedagogy of the Oppressed* (1970), were the half-breed, the matutos, caboclos, lighter than black, darker than white, the product of the colonial rape, the fruit of natives and slaves, or as Wolf (1982) puts it, the people without history. Freire was from the Brazilian northeast, the most oppressed, poorest region in the country. It is the dry land, from where the nordestinos have historically migrated to the south looking for survival. Brazilians in the southern regions welcome the cheap labor, but blame the *nordestinos* for all the social problems, calling them the lazy short people with big heads, darker than white, but not quite as black as the cool African black of carnival, soccer, and music lore. Freire himself was a hybrid white body, in Bhabha's hybridity concept, not only as the "acceptable and regulated" mix of races, forced mostly through rape and destructive systems of domination, but a mixing that goes beyond the biological and scientific constraints. Borrowing from Bhabha (1994),

> Hybridity is the sign of the productivity of colonial power, its shifting forces and fixities; it is the name for the strategic reversal of the process of domination through disavowal (that is the production of discriminatory identities that secure the "pure" and original identity of authority). Hybridity is the revaluation of the assumption of colonial identity through the repetition of discriminatory identity effects. It displays the necessary deformation and displacement of all sites of discrimination and domination. It unsettles the mimetic or narcissistic demands of colonial power but reimplicates its identifications in strategies of subversion that turn the gaze of the discriminated back upon the eye of the power.
>
> *(p. 112)*

Freire and his cultural workers risked their lives in their mission to help the oppressed in how to "read the world." He had to leave Brazil after the 1964 military coup in order not to lose his life. Exile, forced migration, diasporas are not invitations. They are exclusionary impositions based on essentializing notions and labeling of others. To be sure, we are aware of some of Freire's shortcomings in issues of gender, race, etc. But aren't we all some kind of – with variations – product of our own historical and political time? Isn't Freire's statement that only the oppressed can liberate the oppressed very close to the principles of Black feminism thought? There are no leaders in this revolution. So because one is white s/he cannot be a part of the decolonizing project? Or do we have to claim the skin color of a darker grandfather to prove that we belong in the decolonial imaginary? We support and cherish many versions of decolonizing imaginations, but we do not accept essentializing representations and labeling as part of liberatory decolonization. We must reject essentialist ontological binaries, for they have been the "masters' tools" (Lorde, 1984) of colonization and oppression, and find our way toward *inclusive* and *cooperative* emancipation from our colonial history.

Our world is no longer divided between natives and settlers. It may have never been that static, clear-cut, or fixed. For decolonization to happen, the most relevant focus has to be on the power differential between the more dominant and the more subservient peoples, not on any particular flattened, prescribed ontological category. In this historical context, liberation needs to happen first at the "internal" and "mental" levels that essentialist approaches seem to dismiss (Barker, 2011; Tuck & Yang, 2012). Like Paulo Freire, many scholars who speak from their betweenness against varying forms of essentialist ontologies and epistemologies find a common cause in the fight against ideologies of domination and the systems of oppression, exclusion, and privilege that domination constructs, maintains, and guards. We find solace, hope, and inspiration in the notions of decolonization that work toward healing, unity, and cooperation among all peoples of the planet, not on proclamations of exclusion and new diasporas.

Instead of more essentialist representations and interpretations of lived experience in our globalized postcolonial times, we are looking for narratives of lives lived, here and there, in the spaces *between* fixed identities. We are looking for embodied performances that speak to bodies living in postcolonial situations of injustice and are starving for "intensely sensuous way of knowing" (Conquergood, 1991, p. 180). Freire's work gives us that possibility. Scholars writing and teaching from the spaces in-between identities give us that possibility. Betweener autoethnographies give us that possibility.

Borders, legacies, and injustices must be transgressed
Our betweener bodies must be transgressive as a form of scholarship
We feel the duty
To manipulate and transform
The tale of colonization
Using our lives as a source to show
With a political purpose
Experiences in and of the in-between
The aim is to expand the sacredness of life
Beyond essentializing borders

7
TRAVELING IDENTITIES

Here we examine current debates about identity politics and the persistence of exclusionary narratives through reflections that Marcelo has had about embracing our traveling identities as a common ground for conversations and imaginations about decolonizing possibilities.

"You look just like my sister," Emily reads off her paper. She tells us how her androgynous ethnicity has allowed her to experience "breathtaking moments of intimacy and connection" with Others from Other-lands, while at the same time confusing fellow Americans so keen on pinpointing her identity into some recognizable category of race.

Emily ends her performance of *Performing Brown* and that small room on the fourth floor of the Illini Union lets out a sigh. To me, it was a breathtaking performance of decolonizing utopia. She travels in identities as conscientiously as she travels in the developing world gathering stories of human rights violations – using her androgynous ethnicity to advance intimacy and connection with Others, not to subjugate them as characters of her scholarly and journalistic performances.

But, again to me, the most powerful resonance comes from the shift from our obsession with "identi-fication" to the possibilities of connection with the Other through the very blurriness traditional identity politics seeks to eliminate and clarify via reductionist categories. She finishes her performance without giving us names to make sense of her ethnicity.

"You spend the entire paper talking about your hybrid ethnicity and its centrality in the human interactions you have made across the Third World countries you visited as a journalist. Yet you never tell us your ethnicity. It's like a tease," an audience member comments at the end of Emily's *Performing Brown*.

"My intent is not to tease for the sake of cultivating a mysterious persona, but to intentionally punctuate our obsession with fixed categories of race. I want to create narratives of inclusiveness, where people are connected by their common humanity and not separated by clarifying the boundaries of ethnicity or race," Emily replies.

At the risk of having distorted her words, I believe Emily's elegant response proposes a type of narrative of possibilities that can help us move past the lingering essentialism within self-proclaimed liberal scholarship and activism – where the privileged is casually bashed as if "they" were all monolithic zombies feeding on "our" flesh, where Third World scholars are assumed to be indigenous representatives of "their" oppressed people, where postcolonial scholars demand high fees and limousines to come to our campuses with messages of resistance toward the culture of consumption and the neoliberal logic of late capitalism.

The journey toward inclusiveness, however, must be paved by an ever increasing attention to, and reflexivity about, our tendencies to see the Other through identity politics. I believe we can't avoid this human condition. Instead, I believe we need to become more aware of our own identity politics via a never-ending process of conscientização (Freire, 1970). And in my view, narratives of betweenness, of lives experienced in-between the desire to be treated as fully human and the demonizing representations of ourselves by those with more structural privilege, offers powerful possibilities about how to interact with the Other using identity politics as an *inclusive* communicative strategy.

I know I could use the help...

Earlier in the day I had asked Hari where he was from.

"Massachusetts," he said, without hesitation or haste.

"Right on," I said back.

But in my mind I said, "And before Massachusetts?"

Hari's facial expression was still friendly and warm. But he didn't budge before my pushy silence.

"Right on," I said again, "and how do you like living there?" What a lame question to ask someone who just told you he is from that state. He gave me some generic response and I could tell he was trying to let me off the hook.

"I hear you, man," I wanted to tell him, "I've also refused to pin down my identity to a more acceptable place." But to say it out loud would be to announce that I didn't believe he was from Massachusetts. A bad way to connect with someone I was trying to befriend.

In the act of a few warm-up words, I had unwittingly placed myself in the thick of identity politics. And to my dismay, I had placed myself in the very position I tend to criticize – that of a little box demanding to be dealt with in dichotomous ways, a yes-or-no approach to one of the most complex human experiences; that is, who we are. Such is the fragility and inadequacy of our communicative strategies and performances, even when one explicitly embraces decolonizing ideals of treating and thinking of the Other based centrally on the content of his or her character, like someone famous in America dreamt of a few decades ago.

I, too, have been asked the same question for more than 25 years, ever since moving to the United States from Brazil. Why isn't my skin more, uh, ethnic? You must have played soccer growing up, right? How come your accent in English sounds different from the way Mexicans sound? What do you mean Spanish is not your native language? How come you have blue eyes? And, in the spirit of autoethnography that examines lived experience from as many perspectives as I can manage to engage, I have been surprised by how similar the questions have been across the various subcultures with which I have interacted in my decades of life in America.

I have often made things worse by trying to use humor as an evasive strategy of communicative connection with a new acquaintance. On such occasions, I must have thought that perhaps I could use humor to show that I want to connect with the new person while also hiding the mild irritation of having to explain my identity, again. But more often than not, my prosaic humor has had the unintended effect of deflating the initial overtures at meaningful connection. For instance, I used to answer the question about my blue eyes by saying that I wear blue contact lenses. Obviously, I rarely got the easy laughter I aimed for. So the deflating reactions I mostly got must have been due to annoyance at my clear evasiveness, a certain repulsion that I would be so vain as to jeopardize my eyes by inserting two synthetic discs against two of my most precious and delicate body parts for the sake of appearance, or any number of other reactions that I was unable to identify but that, without a doubt, had no strings attached to humor. Also clear to me is that the sudden thickness in the atmosphere of the conversation is largely due to the grip of identity politics in everyday life, however recluse a community strives to be. So much so that we are often at a loss about how to express our intention of inclusiveness, most of us too aware of the potential mis-identity minefields ready to be triggered with each utterance.

Identity politics. It has been oppressively pervasive throughout recorded and performed history. Postcolonialism and affiliated schools of thought have made great strides in troubling the universal acceptance of ideologies of domination that justify, in the name of higher moral grounds or plain tribal impetus, the exclusion and dehumanization of the Other/Different. Yet, it is my perception that most of us decolonizing scholars still lack the language and sociological imagination to incorporate larger-scale decolonizing critique into our everyday interactions with Others. The intention behind my question to Hari, about his geopolitical origin, may be good. And if my social skills can be trusted, I can say that the intentions fueling the questions about my identity location (via the color of my eyes, skin, and accent) have been overwhelmingly about positive connection.

Yet we stumble, on all sides.

Recently, and in lieu of the current economic recession and widespread budget cuts, a group of faculty members at my small satellite state university campus got together to draft a letter of statement urging the administration to be mindful of the lack of diversity among the faculty body. The message was straightforward and familiar across campuses in the United States:

> One of the central missions of a university is to promote inclusiveness and diversity of thought and bodies. Our faculty body grossly under-represents students, staff, and faculty of minority segments of the national and local population. We cannot take backward steps in our pursuit of diversity beyond theoretical constructs. Don't lay off workers of minority standings. We are watching as you lobby at the legislature on the university's behalf.

Then, with the letter drafted and circulated among the faculty of 70 or so, I receive a personalized request to sign it, to make a statement, to voice my support for my own people.

My own people.

Identity politics.

Be careful, I hear myself thinking.

How do I navigate this everyday minefield? As a decolonizing scholar, I support the identity politics fueling the letter. I am inspired to see colleagues with structural privilege pick this battle with a system that continues to exclude obvious minorities. Yet, I find myself in a peculiar position in this ethnic strife. If I sign it, I will feel deceitful, even if I never get found out. If I don't sign it, I will likely be perceived as spineless by well-intentioned peers going out on a limb for me.

An email exchange follows.

> April 28, 2009, 4:04 PM
>
> Marcelo,
>
> I agree this letter is an unnecessary risk, but it does raise the question… what would be a necessary risk for Dr. Diversi? As a man of privilege – what Audre Lorde referred to as the "mythical norm" – I'm allowed to ask such pompous questions! I'm not expecting an answer though… that would be truly pompous.
>
> Signed: Professor "White Heterosexual Tenured Male"

> April 28, 2009, 4:33 PM
>
> Dear Professor "White Heterosexual Tenured Male,"
>
> For us it is a necessary unrisk. They have to deal with us. When I made tenure, the Provost came by later that same day and said "I just wanted to meet the new guy." I had been here six damn years at that point but now he knew he had to deal with me. Privilege is structural, not mythical. And I don't see a lot of tenured Audre Lorde types at faculty meetings.
>
> Signed: Professor "Another White Heterosexual Tenured Male"

> April 29, 2009, 8:56 PM
>
> Dear colleagues!

My main concern wasn't about my own neck being at risk here – though, of course, the risk of retaliation from top dogs rang plenty of bells. Signing a letter that singles out support for diversity among non-tenured faculty strikes a powerful self-serving cord to me, as one of the non-tenured faculty unnamed in the letter. The other significant reason for not signing the letter is that I am not knowledgeable enough about its origin, history, and development to make a more informed decision. I didn't even know, until you two explained earlier this week, that the true audience for the letter was the top administration. My ignorance about the micro-level workings of budgetary political systems led me to think the letter was to continue to apply pressure on the legislators. Keeping our own top administrators to the fire didn't even occur to me, which also exposes my ignorance of our internal representational politics. I didn't realize such move was needed! And I didn't know about prop I-200 (had to look that up, actually... shocking how they spun the wording of the prop to leave out affirmative action!). I ordered Sister Outsider and look forward to reading The Master's Tool Will Never Dismantle the Master's House in its original version for the first time. So for that, too, I am thankful you both have engaged me in this conversation.

Lest I misguide you two about my idiosyncratic stance on diversity and privilege, I must come out to you. I am talking about being a betweener in the intersections of race, ethnicity, and minority status. I, too, am a man of privilege in my own betweeness: skin not quite dark, more smiles than raised chin, lazy revolutionary, and a male WASC (Catholic variation of your WASP) for the first 23 years of my life. Well, not so much Catholic in a theological sense. And perhaps exactly for that, I grew up and continue to be among the most privileged in Brazil since the end of monarchy. To add insult to injury, I was an excellent soccer player. Heterosexual, too. The absurd irony is that I may trump the privileges of the so-called White Heterosexual American Male, as I double my privileged stance by ripping the benefits of my apparent minority status as a Latino in American academia. So, there. Complicated, sure. Nonetheless, my own hybrid identity, and the unearned privileges I have experienced throughout my life, form a powerful reason for my not wanting to sign the letter (or rock the boat when my friendly Latinoness is exploited by the Marketing department's insistence in moving my larger than life picture from billboard to billboard around town). I benefit from the structure AND the myth. There is more. But I will stop here before becoming the lamb who hands the knife to the butcher. I try my hardest not to abuse my privileged betweeness. Not signing the letter was a symbolic act in this spirit (albeit small and inconsequential, to be sure).

For whatever it's worth to you at this point, know that I appreciate and support the progressive agenda behind this letter. I too dream of the day visceral knowledge of oppression informs knowledge production as colleagues and not only as objects of study.

Signed: Marcelo

April 30, 2009, 10:54 AM
Marcelo,
I greatly appreciate the effort you made to explain some of this to me. Not having ever experienced betweeness, I can't really understand, or even imagine, the potential contradictions. Whenever I am faced with an ethnicity menu and I see all the choices and gradations of other like "non-white Hispanic" I feel like a man in a safe house watching a storm. Nothing I have to make decisions about personally, but I sense a lot of turmoil over there and most often look away. So I apologize for assuming that the only reason not to sign the letter was that you are not tenured.

Nonetheless, on our campus, the ins and the outs are rather clear cut. If the opposite of privilege is vulnerability, then there is not much betweeness about it, rather a distinct dualism, tenured or non-tenured. On our campus, that dualism correlates very heavily with race, not just in our college, but in every college. Our junior faculty is a far more diverse group than our senior faculty. The difference is very stark, even if you start educating me about betweeness. The national article that led to the drafting of this letter indicated that this was true nationally and that junior faculty cut backs would skew heavily toward people of color. To me, this puts the lie to the notion that the tenured are where they are simply because they have earned it. And injustice requires a response… blah blah blah, you know the rest.

Signed: Professor "Another White Heterosexual Tenured Male"

This exchange is an instantiation of an inherent predicament of the decolonizing school of thought: standpoint politics. Who gets to say what is decolonizing scholarship? Who can say who the Other is? Is it he who publishes texts with words like postcolonial and decolonizing? Is it she who coined decolonizing terms and words? Is it us who claim to do scholarship that advances unconditional inclusiveness? How do we both claim to be "pro" something while avoiding being "con" those with differing opinions and views?

I am not sure if these questions are even relevant to others. But grounded as I am in my own standpoint, I think we, decolonizing scholars, can't move toward greater inclusiveness without becoming more well versed about our own binary impulses to label the world in crisp categories – and our impulse to claim a superior ideology.

8

ACTIVISM THROUGH DECOLONIZING INQUIRY

Self-righteous
  Political
  Biased
  Subjective
  Inappropriate
  Unscientific
  Emotional
  Distorted
  And our (least) favorite: Pretentious

Calling yourself an activist is pretentious, we hear now and then. Equating academic activism with pretension baffles us. Even more so because it comes from people we expect, hope, to be our allies in the larger project of imagining a world with less suffering and more justice for more people. Unless one teaches and produces knowledge with the single aim to fulfill personal satisfaction, why not embrace the activist ideal, that of working for the greater good? How can this be pretentious, or presumptuous, or self-righteous?

Surely, activism is many things: agitation, hacktivism, campaigning, boycotts, propaganda, strikes, protests. Activism can be silent, though it is generally loud.

It can be inclusionary, exclusionary, or one pretending to be the other. Surely, activism can be misguided.

Marcelo: I am sure I have been misguided in my own activism.
Claudio: I am sure I have been misguided in my own activism.
We have certainly been misguided,
by our blind spots,
by our positionality,
by our idiosyncrasies,

by the inevitable distortions of our passion
by the limitations of our abilities, especially the limitations we don't recognize
by a gaze that can only see the world from the "somewhere" we inhabit
by believing, most days, that what we do as educators and scholars matter more than it might

But even the valid fear of misguided activism does not justify, in our view, casting a shadow of suspicion on the ideal and concept itself. Keeping one of the most hopeful human sentiments and acts out of the academic pursuit seems, to us, like serious folly. Why leave out, be suspicious of, the very human invention that can help us deal with the ideologies of domination that have plagued our history, plague our present, threaten our future?

We are more than 7 billion on a spinning ball of clay, collectively consuming more than the planet can sustain while still making conditions livable for us, with privilege so high that some of us can afford to sign up for leisure space travel, side by side with hardship so mighty that some of us perish in starvation, thirst, cold, war, and endless variations of violence. And we are headed toward an even more crowded planet, with an ever increasing addiction to energy and consumption of things. The persistent problems of exclusion, inequality, and persecution continue. Anyone living in the USA, or paying attention to the news here in recent years, is aware of the persistent police brutality against Black men. Those paying attention are aware that women still make 78 cents to the male dollar, aware that this number gets significantly worse for women of color. The list of inequalities and injustices continues to be too long despite our tantalizing technological advances. Education and knowledge production, we hope, has to serve for us, the human race, to find ways to ease the pain we inflict on ourselves, on each other, on our living home.

For those who want an activism-free academia, we hope you see the light one day. We hope that your work manages to find a way of serving the greater good despite yourself. In the very least, we hope you don't become a hypocrite and trouble the rest of us with being an activist against academic activism.

Marcelo: Yes, I am thinking of you, my university colleague who says we should find ways to legally screen against activists during the hiring process.

Claudio: Yes, I am thinking of you, my colleague who considers activism in academia an inappropriate use of state resources.

Marcelo: Yes, we are thinking of you, colleagues who continue to insist that the right method will set the personal free from the political, that the right paradigm will give you a valid excuse to pretend your "I," your positionality, does not color your words, texts, lectures, body, and work.

Claudio: Dear detached objective colleague, next time you have the urge to criticize academic activism, please go back to the historical context of your own paradigm and do some studying. You will see that the rise of logical positivism was an activist reaction against dogma and totalitarian control of knowledge, its production, and its application to everyday life.

Marcelo: Dear apolitical colleague, next time you equate activism with unreasonable partiality, please go brush up on your understanding of neutrality. You will see that being apolitical in the university and knowledge production only means compliance with the status quo. And the status quo is unequal, unjust, and unsustainable from an environmental perspective.

We look back in history and see that we have been able to make much progress exactly because of activism, of working for and toward the greater good. We no longer sanction burning heretics alive in public squares because, with all of our human flaws, some of our sisters and brothers across history and geopolitical boundaries embraced the notion of working for the greater good. And this work has happened and must continue to happen also inside universities and scholarship. The way we see it, every educator is an activist. Every scholar is an activist. The way we see it, the danger is not in embracing activism, but in the illusion that not being one is possible for symbolic beings like us, humans. The danger is NOT to be aware of how one is exercising activism in the classroom, writing, hiring, firing, or even apparently mundane faculty meetings.

We stand on the strong shoulders of courageous activist-scholars:
bell hooks
Gloria Anzaldúa
Paulo Freire
Norman Denzin
Edward Said
Omi Osun
Franz Fanon
Noam Chomsky
Soyini Madison
Emma Perez
Bryant Alexander
Cherrie Moraga
Mary Weems
So many others

Educators/activists laboring in academic settings where the line that separates scholarship and activism (and vice versa) is
Non-existent!

D. Soyini Madison, in her book *Acts of Activism: Human Rights as Radical Performance* (2010) notes that the fight for human rights involves the use of public space, where a "public space is a promise of a democratic space" (p. 6), and the inclusion of politics – power – and the work of activism itself into the body: "Embodiment. These tactical and emergent performances encourage an embodied epistemology. They become a transformation of knowledge that literally *moves* our musculature and rhythms of our breath and heart, as a corporeal knowledge conjoins through enfleshment knowledge" (p. 7). That's at the center of our performances, written and embodied, the use of our bodies in educational public spaces challenging, disrupting, resisting structures and powers of oppression. Our knowledge production, our theorizing of the flesh (Moraga and Anzaldúa, 1981), our bodies in the line, in the public, institutional, pedagogical space of classrooms.

Activism is central to decolonizing inquiry, and vice versa. We embrace decolonizing inquiry as a framework to imagine a future we will never see, but that we hope will be kinder, more collaborative, ever more inclusionary. We lean on decolonizing inquiry to inform the activism we bring to our classrooms, texts, performances, and praxis. To us, decolonizing inquiry is founded on a search for ways of placing Western epistemology at the end of the researcher's gaze. Decolonizing inquiry makes Western systems of knowledge production the very objects of study about social justice, injustice, and the persistent ideologies of domination of our times (Denzin, 2005, p. 936). This inward gaze is an act of activism in and of itself.

Again, we might have been misguided in our activism along the way. So we constantly attempt to bring activism to the classroom, our texts and performances, while at the same time questioning our assumptions and preconceptions. We search for ways to strengthen our alignment with the basic principle that education and knowledge production have to help us understand and challenge the ideologies of domination of our times, so we can then imagine and debate and imagine, over and over, a more inclusive future. Guided by the principles of solidarity, inclusion, humanization, caring, and hope, we attempt to bring activism to every class we teach, every course we prepare, every new group of students we meet.

We believe that activism is in the attempt to connect the classroom to history, the personal to the political (Lorde, 1984), the individual troubles to public issues (Mills, 1959). Activism, to us, is the hyperawareness that the attempt to be apolitical in education and scholarship leads to replication of the status quo, to the reification of the inequalities and stratification of the greater world reflected in academia. Activism in academia, to us, is to deconstruct, over and over, the binaries that insist on privileging theory over lived experience, expert over subject, men over women, European over indigenous civilizations, fixed over fluid identities. We all know the story of privilege. Even "apolitical" academics tend to acknowledge how the many disparities of society are represented in universities.

So, though it may seem pretentious to some, we bring our protest signs and hybrid bodies to the front of our performance texts and the stage of the classroom. We bring our half-breed mutt-like bodies to the forefront to try and break the dichotomy of the personal and political, to break the revolving notion that activism is appropriate only outside the classroom and scholarship. As academic activists, we invite students and colleagues to become border smugglers of identities against fixed notions about geographies and cultures, against tidy representations of self and the Other. We might be misguided in our activism at times. But we are clear about its absolute importance for the academic project to be worthwhile.

Words to End With

> Themness, this sense that some people are not fully human and not to be trusted is no longer a passing thought. It leaves the realm of psychology and becomes a political fact. Some of the myriad human kinds you see, then, feel as if they are not, never were, never could be, part of the human community. Their misery, then, does not feel like human misery. Their blood flowing in the gutter is not human blood.
>
> (Berreby, 2008, p. 222)

The debate about the origins and universality of ideologies of domination is complex, politically charged, and a topic for a different place and time. Here we want to end with an appeal to the possibilities for a decolonizing imaginary for our future (Diversi & Moreira, 2009; Perez, 1999), where ever more people can experience a world of much greater inclusiveness than the present one. And, at least in our experience of the world, a significant barrier is our lack of language and imagination about how to advance unconditional inclusiveness while experiencing repulsion toward Others – because of their politics, looks, styles, lesser morals, and so on – on a daily basis. To resolve this internal contradiction, we create elaborate rationalizations to justify our higher moral ground, as the alternative, hypocrisy, would be too threatening to admit. We think that exploring human experiences of identity betweenness, of living in-between worlds, of living in nepantla, *la tierra entre medio*, the land between known places and identities (Anzaldúa, 1987/1999), offers a hopeful alternative to such rationalizations of exclusion by asking that we find common ground in our search for dignity, by embracing the traveling nature of our identities – and by intentionally resisting impulses to anchor identities, our own as well as Others', against fixed labels, in particular against labels that make people's identities and humanity so distant from ours that we become unable to feel our inescapable human connection. Our fate in living and surviving in peace on an overpopulated planet, based on energy and economic policies that are depleting the earth's natural resources and disrupting its ecological systems more rapidly than natural replenishment can happen, with technology that is both massively deadly and relational across a multitude of human tribes, depends on our collective ability to decrease and humanize the spaces between Us and Them, between supremacist ideologists.

Moving past our historical and universal obsession with linking personal and group identity to human worth and belonging may not be possible. But the attempt will certainly require more than masterful theorizing. And here is where betweener autoethnographies can contribute to decolonizing narratives that promote a pedagogy of hope and inclusion. Textual performances can be created by betweeners grounded in the various realms of identity politics of our everyday lives: ethnicity, nationality, sexuality, family, struggles for inclusion and against exclusion, Others, home, and so on. Betweener stories and storytellers can embody the hope that one day the Other will join the postcolonial movement as gatherers and tellers of decolonizing narratives. Scholarly representation and narratives that challenge binary (either/or) and fixed identity politics, where one's full humanity becomes flattened into a stereotype of the demonized Other (e.g., Donald Trump's notion that Mexicans are rapists and Muslims are terrorists), can embody the very hope of a decolonizing utopia where identity politics can be used to expand the circle of inclusion, not to morally justify exclusion and violence toward the Other. Narratives of traveling identities answer the call for qualitative inquiry that advances social justice (Denzin & Giardina, 2009), methodologies of the heart (Pelias, 2004), decolonizing knowledge production (Sandoval, 2000; Weems, 2003), writing liberating cultural plots (Min-ha, 1989), and self-reflexive conscientização (Freire, 1970). May we all become teachers and decolonizing performers furthering possibilities for the next generation of dreamers.

REFERENCES

Adams, T. E., Holman Jones, S. & Ellis, C. (2015). *Autoethnography*. New York: Oxford University Press.
Adichie, C. N. (2009). The danger of a single story. Filmed at TEDGlobal, July. Retrieved from www.ted.com/talks/chimamanda_adichie_the_danger_of_a_single_story/tra nscript?language=en#t-291968
Alexander, B. K. (1999). Performing culture in the classroom: An instructional (auto) ethnography. *Text and Performance Quarterly*, 19, 307–331.
Alexander, B. K. (2005). Performance ethnography: The reenacting and inciting of culture. In N. K. Denzin & Y. S. Lincoln (Eds), *Handbook of Qualitative Research* (pp. 411–442). Thousand Oaks, CA: Sage.
Alexander, B. K. (2012). *The performative sustainability of race: Reflections on Black culture and the politics of identity*. New York: Peter Lang.
Anzaldúa, G. (1981). La Prieta. In C. Moraga and G. Anzaldúa (Eds), *This bridge called my back: Writings by radical women of color*. New York: Kitchen Table, Women of Color Press.
Anzaldúa, G. (1987/1999). *Borderlands: The new mestiza = La Frontera* (2nd Ed.). San Francisco, CA: Aunt Lute Books.
Anzaldúa, G. (2000). *Interviews/Entrevistas*. Ed. A. L. Keating. New York: Routledge.
Arjana, S. R. (2015). *Muslims in the Western imagination*. New York: Oxford University Press.
Barker, A. J. (2011). What does 'Decolonize Oakland' mean? What can 'Decolonize Oakland' mean? *Tequila Sovereign*. Retrieved from http://tequilasovereign.blogspot.ca/2011/10/whatdoes-decolonize-oakland-mean-what.html
Baldwin, J. (1979). Interview by Mel Atkins. *New York Times Book Review*, September 23, 3.
Baldwin, J. & Mead, M. (1974). *Rap on race*. New York: Random House Publishing.
Benjamin, W. (1968). *Illuminations*. Ed. H. Arendt. Trans. H. Zohn. New York: Harcourt.
Berreby, D. (2008). *Us & them: The science of identity*. Chicago, IL: University of Chicago Press.

References

Bhabha, H. K. (1994). *The location of culture*. London: Routledge.
Bochner, A. & Ellis, C. (2016). *Evocative autoethnography: Writing lives and telling stories*. New York: Routledge.
Butler, J. (1993). *Bodies that matter: On the discursive limits of sex*. London: Routledge.
Chomsky, N. (1999). *Profit over people: Neoliberalism and the global order*. New York: Seven Stories Press.
Chomsky, N. (2005). *Imperial ambitions: Conversation on the post-9/11 world*. New York: Metropolitan Books.
Clarke, J., Hall, S., Jefferson, T., & Roberts, B. (2006). Subcultures, cultures and class. In S. Hall & T. Jefferson (Eds), *Resistance through rituals: Youth subcultures in post-war Britain* (pp. 3–59). New York: Routledge.
Clifford, J. & Marcus, G. (1986). *Writing culture: The poetics and politics of ethnography*. Los Angeles, CA: University of California Press.
Clough, P. T. (1994). *Feminist thought*. Cambridge, MA: Blackwell.
Coates, T. (2017). *We were eight years in power: An American tragedy*. London: One World.
Conquergood, D. (1991). Rethinking ethnography: Towards a critical cultural politics. *Communications Monographs*, 58, 178–194.
Conquergood, D. (2002). Performance studies: Interventions and radical research. *TDR: The Drama Review*, 46, 137–141.
Crittenden, P. (1998). The singular universal in Jean-Paul Sartre. *Literature & Aesthetics*, 8, 29–42.
Darder, A. (2002). *Reinventing Paulo Freire: A pedagogy of love*. Boulder, CO: Westview.
Deloria, V. (1969). *Custer died for your sins: An Indian manifesto*. New York: Macmillan.
Denzin, N. (1997). *Interpretive ethnography: Ethnographic practices for the 21st century*. Thousand Oaks, CA: Sage.
Denzin, N. K. (2003). *Performance ethnography: Critical pedagogy and the politics of culture*. Thousand Oaks, CA: Sage.
Denzin, N. K. (2005). Emancipatory discourses and the ethics and politics of interpretation. In N. Denzin & Y. Lincoln (Eds), *Handbook of qualitative research* (pp. 933–958). Thousand Oaks, CA: Sage.
Denzin, N. K. (2009). Critical pedagogy and democratic life or a radical democratic critical pedagogy and democratic life or a radical democratic. *Cultural Studies ⊠ Critical Methodologies*, 9, 379–397.
Denzin, N. K. (2010). *The qualitative manifesto: A call to arms*. Walnut Creek, CA: Left Coast Press.
Denzin, N. K. (2013). *Interpretive autoethnography* (2nd Ed.). Thousand Oaks, CA: Sage.
Denzin, N. K. & Giardina, M. D. (Eds). (2009). *Qualitative inquiry and social justice: Toward a politics of hope*. Walnut Creek, CA: Left Coast Press.
Denzin, N. K. & Giardina, M. D. (2013). *Global dimensions of qualitative inquiry*. Walnut Creek, CA: Left Coast Press.
Denzin, N. & Lincoln, Y. (1994). *Handbook of qualitative research*. Thousand Oaks, CA: Sage.
Derrida, J. (1967/2016). *Of grammatology*. Trans. G. C. Spivak, Introduction J. Butler. Baltimore, MD: Johns Hopkins University Press.
Dimitriadis, G. & McCarthy, C. (2000). Stranger in the village: James Baldwin, popular culture, and the ties that bind. *Qualitative Inquiry*, 6, 171–187.
Diversi, M. (1998). Glimpses of street life: Representing lived experience through short stories. *Qualitative Inquiry*, 4, 131–147.

Diversi, M. (2014). Damming the Amazon: The postcolonial march of the wicked West. *Cultural Studies ⊠ Critical Methodologies*, 14, 242–246.
Diversi, M. & Henhawk, D. (2012). Indigenous qualitative inquiry: (Re)awakening, together, from a long colonizing slumber. *International Review of Qualitative Research*, 5, 51–72.
Diversi, M. & Moreira, C. (2009). *Betweener talk: A dialogue on decolonizing class, knowledge production, pedagogy, and praxis*. Walnut Creek, CA: Left Coat Press.
Diversi, M. & Moreira, C. (2012). Decolonizing constructions of childhood and history: Interrupting narratives of avoidance to children's questions about social injustice. *International Journal of Qualitative Studies in Education*, 25, 189–203.
Domonoske, C. (2016). NPR, refugees, displaced people surpass 60 million for first time, UNHCR says. *NPR*. Retrieved from www.npr.org/sections/thetwo-way/2016/06/20/482762237/refugees-displaced-people-surpass-60-million-for-first-time-unhcr-says
Douglas, K. & Carless, D. (2013). A history of autoethnographic inquiry. In S. H. Jones, T. E. Adams, & C. Ellis (Eds), *Handbook of authoethnography* (pp. 84–106). Thousand Oaks, CA: Left Coast Press.
Douglass, F. (1845/2003). *Narrative of the life of Frederick Douglass: An American slave*. New York: Barnes & Noble's Classics.
Douglass, F. (1855). *My bondage and my freedom*. New York: Miller, Orton, & Mulligan.
Douglass, F. (1881). *Life and times of Frederick Douglass*. Hartford, CT: Park Publishing.
Durham, A. (2010). *On getting tenure*. Spotlight panel. VI International Congress of Qualitative Inquiry, May. Champaign, IL: University of Illinois at Urbana-Champaign.
Ellis, C. (2004). *The ethnographic I: A methodological novel about teaching and doing autoethnography*. Walnut Creek, CA: Altamira Press.
Fanon, F. (1952/2008). *Black skin, white masks*. Trans. R. Philcox). New York: Grove Press.
Fanon, F. (1963/2004). *The wretched of the earth*. Trans. R. Philcox. New York: Grove Press.
Fausto, B. (1996). *Historia do Brasil*. São Paulo: Editora da Universidade de São Paulo.
Federal Elections Commission (2017). *Official 2016 Presidential general election results*. Washington, DC: U.S. National Archives and Records Administration.
Freire, P. (1970). *Pedagogy of the oppressed*. Trans. M. Bergman Ramos. New York: Continuum.
Freire, P. (1985). *The politics of education: Culture, power, and liberation*. Trans. D. Macedo. Hadley, MA: Bergin & Garvey.
Freire, P. (1998a). *Pedagogy of freedom: Ethics, democracy, and civic courage*. Trans. P. Clarke. Lanham, MD: Rowman & Littlefield.
Freire, P. (1998b). *Pedagogy of the heart*. Trans. D. Macedo and A. Oliveira, Foreword M. Carnoy). New York: Continuum.
Freire, P. (1995). *A sombra desta mangueira*. São Paulo: Olho d'Agua.
Freire, P. (1995/2004). *Pedagogy of hope: Reliving pedagogy of the oppressed*. Trans. R. R. Barr. New York: Continuum.
Freire, P. & Macedo, D. (1987). *Literacy: Reading the word and the world*. South Hadley, MA: Bergin & Garvey.
Garoian, C. (1999). *Performing pedagogy: Toward an art of politics*. Albany, NY: State University of New York Press.
Geertz, C. (1973). *The interpretation of cultures*. New York: Basic Books.
Giardina, M. D. & Denzin, N. K. (2012). Policing the "Penn State Crisis": Violence, power, and the neoliberal university. *Cultural Studies ⊠ Critical Methodologies*, 12, 259–266.

References

Giroux, H. & Giroux, S. S. (2005). Challenging neoliberalism's new world order: The promise of critical pedagogy. *Cultural Studies ⊠ Critical Methodologies*, 6, 21–32.

Goodall, H. L. (2010). *Counter-narrative: How progressive academics can challenge extremists and promote social justice*. Walnut Creek, CA: Left Coast Press.

Grande, S. (2004). *Red pedagogy: Native American social and political thought*. Oxford: Rowman & Littlefield.

Greene, M. (2000). Lived spaces, shared spaces, public spaces. In L. Weis & M. Fine (Eds), *Construction sites: Excavating race, class, and gender among urban youth* (pp. 293–304). New York: Teachers College Press.

Hall, S. (1996). What is this "black" in black popular culture? In D. Morley & K. Chen (Eds), *Stuart Hall: Critical dialogues in cultural studies* (pp. 465–475). London: Routledge.

Hall, S. (1997). *Representation: Cultural representation and signifying practices*. London: Routledge.

Haraway, D. (1991). *Simians, cyborgs and women: The reinvention of nature*. New York: Routledge.

Hill, R. T. G. (1998). Performance pedagogy across the curriculum. In S. J. Dailey (Ed.), *The future of performance studies: Visions and revisions* (pp. 141–144). Annandale, VA: National Communication Association.

Holman Jones, S. (2005). Autoethnography: Making the personal political. In N. Denzin & Y. Lincoln (Eds), *Handbook of qualitative research* (pp. 763–791). Thousand Oaks, CA: Sage.

Holman Jones, S., AdamsT. E., & Ellis, C. (2013). *The handbook of autoethnography*. New York: Routledge.

hooks, b. (1981). *Ain't I a woman: Black women and feminism*. Boston, MA: South End Press.

hooks, b. (1989). *Talking back: Thinking feminist, thinking Black*. Boston, MA: South End Press.

hooks, b. (1994a). *Outlaw culture*. New York: Routledge.

hooks, b. (1994b). *Teaching to transgress: Education as the practice of freedom*. New York: Routledge.

Huey, A. (2010). America's native prisoners of war. TED.com talk: www.ted.com/talks/lang/eng/aaron_huey.html

Hurston, Z. N. (1935/1990). *Mules and Men*. New York: Harper.

Indian Country (2015). Yankton Sioux lead fight against TransCanada and Keystone XL in South Dakota. *Indian Country Today Media Network*. Retrieved from http://indiancountrytodaymedianetwork.com/2015/01/05/yankton-sioux-lead- fight-against-transcanada-and-keystone-xl-south-dakota-158562

Jones, J. L. (1997). Sista docta: Performance as critique of the academy. *TDR: The Drama Review*, 41, 51–67.

Kincheloe, J. L. & McLaren, P. L. (1994). Rethinking critical theory and qualitative research. In N. K. Denzin & Y. Lincoln (Eds), *Handbook of qualitative research* (pp. 138–157). Thousand Oaks, CA: Sage.

Lorde, A. (1984). *Sister outsider*. New York: Crossing Press.

Madison, D. S. (1998). Performance, personal narratives, and the politics of possibility. In S. J. Dailey (Ed.), *The future of performance studies: Visions and revisions*. Annandale, VA: National Communication Association.

Madison, D. S. (2005). *Critical ethnography: Method, ethics, and performance*. Thousand Oaks, CA: Sage.

Madison, D. S. (2009). Dangerous ethnography. In N. Denzin & M. Giardina (Eds), *Qualitative inquiry and social justice: Toward a politics of hope* (pp. 187–197). Walnut Creek, CA: Left Coast Press.

Madison, D. S. (2010). *Acts of activism: Human rights as radical performance*. Cambridge: Cambridge University Press.

McLaren, P. (2002). Afterword. In A. Darder (Ed.), *Reinventing Paulo Freire: A pedagogy of love*. Boulder, CO: Westview Press.

Mead, M. & Baldwin, J. (1972). *A rap on race*. New York: Dell Publishing.

Merleau-Ponty, M. (1969). *The visible and the invisible*. Evanston, IL: Northwestern University Press.

Mills, C. W. (1959). *The sociological imagination*. New York: Oxford University Press.

Min-ha, T. T. (1989). *Woman, native, other: Writing postcoloniality and feminism*. Bloomington, IN: Indiana University Press.

Moraga, C. & Anzaldúa, G. (1981). *This bridge called my back: Writings by radical women of color*. Watertown, MA: Persephone Press.

Moreira, C. (2008). Fragments. *Qualitative Inquiry*, 14, 663–683.

Moreira, C. & Diversi, M. (2010). When janitors dare to become scholars: A betweeners' view of the politics of knowledge production from decolonizing street-corners. *International Review of Qualitative Research*, 2, 457–474.

Moreira, C. & Diversi, M. (2011). Missing bodies: Troubling the colonial landscape of American academia. *Text and Performance Quarterly*, 31, 229–248.

O'Donnell, J. R. (1991). *Trumped! The inside story of the real Donald Trump: His cunning rise and spectacular fall*. New York: Simon & Schuster.

Pelias, R. J. (2004). *A methodology of the heart: Evoking academic and daily life*. Walnut Creek, CA: Altamira.

Perez, E. (1999). *The decolonial imaginary: Writing Chicanas into history*. Bloomington, IN: Indiana University Press.

Pineau, E. L. (1998). Performance studies across the curriculum: Problems, possibilities and projections. In S. J. Dailey (Ed.), *The future of performance studies: Visions and revision* (pp. 128–135). Annandale, VA: National Communication Association.

Pollock, D. (1998a). A response to Dwight Conquergood's essay "Beyond the text: Towards a performative cultural politics." In S. J. Dailey (Ed.), *The future of performance studies: Visions and revisions* (pp. 37–46). Washington, DC: National Communication Association.

Pollock, D. (1998b). Performing writing. In P. Phelan & J. Lane (Eds), *The ends of performance* (pp. 73–103). New York: New York University Press.

Pollock, D. (1998c). Introduction: Making history go. In D. Pollock (Ed.), *Exceptional spaces: Essays in performance and history* (pp. 1–45). Chapel Hill, NC: University of North Carolina Press.

Pollock, D. (2007). The performative "I." *Cultural Studies ⊠ Critical Methodologies*, 3, 239–255.

Rorty, R. (1979). *Philosophy and the mirror of nature*. Princeton, NJ: Princeton University Press.

Rorty, R. (1999). *Philosophy and social hope*. New York: Penguin.

Said, E. (1978). *Orientalism*. New York: Penguin.

Sandoval, C. (2000). *Methodology of the oppressed*. Minneapolis, MN: University of Minnesota Press.

Sartre, J. P. (1963). *Search for a method*. Trans. H. E. Barnes. New York: Alfred A. Knopf.

Sartre, J. P. (1981). *The family idiot: Gustav Flaubert, Vol. 1, 1821–1857*. Chicago, IL: University of Chicago Press.

Scheper-Hughes, N. (1992). *Death without weeping: The violence of everyday life in Brazil*. Berkeley, CA: University of California Press.

Smith, L. T. (1999). *Decolonizing methodologies: Research and indigenous peoples*. London: Zed Books.

Smith, L. T. (2005). On tricky ground: Researching the native in the age of uncertainty. In N. Denzin & Y. Lincoln (Eds), *Handbook of qualitative research* (3rd Ed.) (pp. 113–143). Thousand Oaks, CA: Sage.

Spry, T. (2011). *Body, paper, stage: Writing and performing autoethnography*. Walnut Creek, CA: Left Coast Press.

Spry, T. (2016). *Autoethnography and the Other: Unsettling power through utopian performances*. New York: Routledge.

Taunay, A. de (1975). *História das bandeiras paulistas* (History of the paulistas' flags) (3rd Ed.). São Paulo: Editora Melhoramentos.

Tuck, E. & Yang, K. W. (2012). Decolonization is not a metaphor. *Decolonization: Indigeneity, Education & Society*, 1, 1–40.

Turner, V. (1986). *The anthropology of performance*. New York: PAJ Publications.

Turner, V. & Bruner, E. (1986). *The anthropology of experience*. Chicago, IL: University of Illinois Press.

Ulmer, G. (1989) *Teletheory: Grammatology in the age of video*. New York: Routledge.

Visweswaran, K. (1994). *Fictions of feminist ethnography*. Minneapolis, MN: University of Minnesota Press.

Weems, M. E. (2003). *Public education and the imagination-intellect: I speak from the wound in my mouth*. New York: Peter Lang.

Wolf, E. R. (1982). *Europe and the people without history*. Berkeley, CA: University of California Press.

Yellow Bird, M. (2004). Cowboys and indians: Toys of genocide, icons of American colonization. *Wicazo Sa Review*, 19, 33–38.

Zinn, H. (1980/2005). *A people's history of the United States: 1492 to present*. New York: Harper Perennial Modern Classics.

INDEX

academic elitism 31, 35–38, 40–57, 60–61, 72, 122, 128; *see also* oppression; systemic exclusion
activism 121–130; *see also* decolonizing inquiry
Alexander, Bryant K. 35, 109
Anzaldúa, Gloria 11, 21–22, 48–49, 54
authenticity 114, 115
authorship, ranking of 37
autoethnography: foundations of 15–18, 110–112; as qualitative inquiry 23–24

Baldwin, James 9, 17–18, 24
being 12
Belo Monte Dam 97–99, 102
biography 17, 63, 109
body(ies) 20, 21–22, 61–73; *see also* historicity; hybridity; identity politics; Other
Brazil, Portuguese 'discovery' of 90–93
Brexit 3

Chambliss, Saxby 85
childhood, constructions of 63–65, 73–74, 90–106
class 27–28, 42, 47–50; *see also* academic elitism
classrooms, as decolonizing sites 83–89
collaborative writing 29–32, 36–37
"collateral damage" 84–85
collectivism 29–32
colonialism/colonization 30, 102, 113; assumptions of 57–59; history 90–93; *see also* hybridity; language use
community, and inclusion 23
Conquergood, Dwight 18–19
conscientization 12, 20–21, 27, 46, 116, 120
consensus, search for 44
critical pedagogy 20–21; and the body 61–73

dam projects, Brazil 97–99, 102
decolonizing essentialism *see* essentialism
decolonizing inquiry 84–106; *see also* activism
decolonizing movement 37, 114; writing within 29–32
decolonizing pedagogies 65–72; *see also* essentialism
deconstructive ethnography 47–48
Denzin, Norman 18, 47–48, 62–63, 95
Dilma *see* Rousseff, Dilma
divergent thinking 21
diversity, as higher education goal 61
Douglass, Frederick 10, 15
drone strikes 84–85
dualisms 35, 76

embodied scholarship 20; *see also* body(ies)
essentialism 59–61, 77, 113–118

Index

ethnic mixing *see* hybridity
exclusion, systemic 39–82; *see also* academic elitism; inclusiveness
expert, lone 32–36

Freire, Paulo 10, 20–21, 27, 41, 43, 46–47, 50–51, 85–86, 115, 116–118

Garoian, C. 62
Greene, Maxine 23, 61
Guantanamo 85

Hall, Stuart 94
healing narratives 22, 80–82
hegemonic cultures, and language 43
higher education, Brazil 28; *see also* academic elitism; knowledge production
Hill, R. T. G. 62
historicity 69, 95, 104
history: and biography 17; decolonizing construction of 90–92, 104; *see also* personal narratives
hooks, bell 18, 52, 84
hope 110
humanism 23, 85, 88
humor 121
hybridity 21, 78, 114, 115, 116–117, 119

identity politics 61, 119–124
immigrants, local 74–76
imperialism 88–89, 92
inclusiveness: as aim 23, 32, 116–118, 120–122; *see also* exclusion, systemic
indigenous peoples 75, 105; Amazon Basin 97–99, 102; historical 90–93
inequalities, children's questions on 94, 96–97
interstitial places 21, 94–95

Jones, Joni 18, 19–20, 49, 60

knowledge production 16, 31, 35–38, 40–53; *see also* academic elitism

language use, in academia/education 39–44; *see also* academic elitism; knowledge production
liberation theologists 15–16
literacy, adult 47
lived experience 45
logical positivism *see* positivism
Lorde, Audre 54, 116

Madison, D. Soyini 127
marginality, and empowerment 23, 94
matutos 105, 117

naming 23
neoliberal narratives 83–90

Obama, Barack 2, 85
ontology 12
oppression: and resistance 62; systems of 15–16, 51–53, 72; visceral knowledge of 11–12, 45–46; *see also* academic elitism
Orlando shooting 4–5
Other 64–65; and the lone expert 32–36; as monster 74, 76, 113; *see also* indigenous peoples

Pacific Northwest, US 74–75
Perez, Emma 21, 22, 94–95
performance 18–20; and the body 61–73, 127–128; decolonizing 59–60
performative critical pedagogy 62–63
performativity, and writing 20, 27–38, 95–96
personal narratives, as critique 15–16
perspective 94
Pineau, E. L. 62, 63
political/personal, the 15, 16
Pollock, Della 19, 20, 34, 38, 95
populist nationalism 2–3, 10
positivism 16, 27, 45, 126
postcolonialism 11, 56, 121
public education, budget-slashing 87
public spaces, reimagining 23, 127–128; *see also* activism
purity 3, 114, 115

qualitative inquiry 15–24

Raoni, Chief 97–98, 102
reconciliation 22, 23
reductionism 58
refugees 3
representation, politics of 55, 111
research, decolonizing 20, 92–93
resistance 23, 62; *see also* activism
revolutionary utopianism 62
Rousseff, Dilma 4, 76, 97–98, 102

Said, Edward 93
Sandusky, Jerry 84
slavery 10, 15

Smith, Linda Tuhiwai 30, 93, 115
social control, and education 42
social justice 1–3, 10–14, 17, 22–24, 28, 30, 41, 50, 102, 111, 128, 130
storytelling, power/politics of 94
supremacy ideologies 2, 16, 23, 129; *see also* Us/Themism
systemic exclusion *see* exclusion, systemic

textbooks, missing bodies in 56
Third World feminism 21–22; *see also* Anzaldúa, Gloria
transformation 62
transgression 90, 118; *see also* activism; resistance
traveling identities 119–124, 129, 130

Trump, Donald 2–4
Tuck, E. 114, 115

Us/Themism 2–3, 12, 22, 23, 75; *see also* supremacy ideologies

violence 4–5, 78, 99–100
visceral knowledge *see under* oppression
Visweswaran, K. 47–48
voyeurism 32

Washington 75
writing, and performativity 20, 27–38, 95–96

Yang, K. W. 114, 115

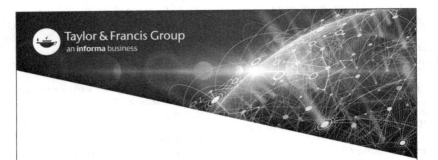

Taylor & Francis eBooks

www.taylorfrancis.com

A single destination for eBooks from Taylor & Francis with increased functionality and an improved user experience to meet the needs of our customers.

90,000+ eBooks of award-winning academic content in Humanities, Social Science, Science, Technology, Engineering, and Medical written by a global network of editors and authors.

TAYLOR & FRANCIS EBOOKS OFFERS:

- A streamlined experience for our library customers
- A single point of discovery for all of our eBook content
- Improved search and discovery of content at both book and chapter level

REQUEST A FREE TRIAL
support@taylorfrancis.com